# SUPER NU
# FOR ANIMAL

by Nina Anderson and Dr. Howard Peiper
& Alicia McWatters, M.S.
**Illustrated by**
Richard Vail & Jeanne Vuyosevich

ISBN 1-884820-16-6-51295
Library of Congress Catalog Card Number 96-70946

Printed in the United States of America


Edited by Rachel Bell

*Super Nutrition for Animals (Birds Too!)* is not intended as medical
advice. It is written solely for informational and educational
purposes. Please consult a health professional should the need for
one be indicated.

Published by Safe Goods
283 East Canaan Rd.
East Canaan, CT 06024
(860)-824-5301

**A percentage of the proceeds from this book will be donated to:**
**BEST FRIENDS ANIMAL SANCTUARY, Kanab, Utah**

→*"Best Friends Animal Sanctuary is delighted to be part of this book and to promote natural health for your pets at home. There are never fewer than fifteen hundred dogs, cats and other animals at the sanctuary. We're well aware of the value of natural health and healing techniques in bringing them back to health and happiness from whatever suffering they may have known.*

*At Best Friends we're always studying holistic approaches to good health, These include good nutrition, extra supplements, homeopathic and flower essences and the best modern veterinary approaches, to chronic medical conditions and acute problems that are causing suffering. We hope that you'll learn some good tips and approaches from this book. Your furry friends here at the sanctuary, wish your animals at home, the very best good health and happiness."*

-Michael Mountain, Editor, Best Friends Magazine

## ACKNOWLEDGEMENTS:

*We would like to thank all the animal lovers that contributed their knowledge in support of this work. The people who offered their humane stories are special, and we commend them for believing that they could find an alternative way to help their animals. We also thank the manufacturers of natural products that have made such a difference, not only in our lives, but in our pets' lives. We would like to express our gratitude to all the scientists, physicians, and researchers who have devoted vast amounts of time in discovering the benefits of nutrients in foods, nutritional supplements, and natural medicine.*

*We give our special thanks to Charlie Fox, Wakunaga Corporation. Without his support and knowledge, this book would not have been completed. James Helfter, Advanced Biological Concepts also receives our gratitude, for providing us with so much necessary information about horses. Jeanne Vuyosevich, Trainer and Breeder of Thoroughbreds, gets special thanks for providing her expertise with natural feeding and treatment of horses. Thomas Willard, Ph.D. also is offered thanks for educating us about ferrets. We also hold in high regard the many aviculturists whose guidance and support made possible, the chapter on birds. We love our pets as special members of the family, and hope we have made the quality of their lives healthier and more enjoyable. We want to thank them for their trust.*

*photo by Neil Shively*

# FORWARD.

Dietary management and nutrition are the foundation of keeping animals healthy and fit. To feed correctly requires a proper understanding of dietary nutrients and their bioavailability.

In the past, animal foods were chosen on the basis of packaging design, advertising claims, cost and convenience. Fortunately, today pet owners are feeding more digestible, higher quality natural pet foods. Because of this, they are being rewarded with animals that look and feel better and may even live longer. However, even high quality premium pet foods may not always be enough to promote optimum health and vitality for every animal.

Each animal, depending on reproductive status, age, temperament and lifestyle has specific and exact nutrient requirements. Fine-tuning animal foods with nutritional supplements provides an integrated and holistic approach to address individual needs. By combining natural foods and conditionally essential vitamins, minerals and enzymes, you can enhance vitality and prevent disease. Super Nutrition For Animals (Birds too!) provides a readily available source of information and assists in better understanding pet diets and proper nutritional balance.

-L. Phillips Brown, D.V.M.
International Marketing Coordinator
Inter-Cal Corporation

# INTRODUCTION.

If you are in the mood for entertaining reading, then you can flip through this book and read the personal stories from folks just like you, who have found a way to heal their pet. If this is as far as you get, you will still receive valuable information. For those who truly want to improve the well being of their four legged or winged family members, we have details on food, nutrition, healing supplements and manufacturers of healthy products. The animals have bugged us for years to do this book, because although they like junk food, they are tired of being sick.

Veterinarians report that many of today's pets suffer from allergies, skin problems, hypertension, heart disease, cancer, liver and kidney failure, to name a few. These conditions have been exaggerated by the "tainted" foods we feed our pets, and the lack of vitamins, enzymes, minerals and other nutrients. There are approximately eighty million pet owners in the United States. These animal lovers spend twenty seven billion dollars on their pets and of that, eleven billion is on food. Advertising in the pet industry is the primary way you hear about their products. Do manufacturers tell you what they put in their cans or boxes? Is it a dead dog or cat? That may sound harsh, but for some manufacturers, it's true. "4D" is a an FDA classification denoting a dead, dying, diseased and disabled meat source. Do they tell you what effect the preservatives and additives may have on your pets health? Of course not! All you see is happy healthy animals lapping up their "yummy" food.

Manufacturers of natural pet foods have lots more conscience. They have provided us with much of their research into what really should be in pet foods and what shouldn't. We have been made aware of the hazards of toxic additives and the need for specific nutrients. Unfortunately even the most trustworthy natural pet food manufacturer, must cook or process foods. Therefore to restore the natural digestibility of the food, supplemental enzymes must be added to the meal. This is one of the focus points covered within the text. There are numerous good books on natural treatments for healing sick pets, and most mention diets, but we go one step further. Information is given on three important features: minerals, enzymes, balancing nutrients.

To make our point, we have included numerous personal stories from pet owners, about the healing power of diets, supplements, natural food and alternative treatments for illness. They are included, not only to entertain you, but to help you make a more educated decision about the future health of your pet. Each story has key words underlined, depicting the animal species, and the health problem that is the focus of the tale. The first chapter outlines nutritional necessities for all species. Please refer back to it when reading about your particular animal interest. These sections are referred to when we talk about ferrets, horses, birds, therefore it is advised that you read them for more comprehensive information. This book is meant to be a starting point for you. Other sources are recommended within the text, to round out your education on specific topics. A Resource Directory is provided as the last chapter. It's purpose is to educate you about products and companies that are dedicated to keeping your pet alive and healthy, naturally. Should your animal be poisoned (from food or toxic substances) you can receive immediate help by calling the National Animal Poison Control Center (800)-548-2423 (charge for service).

Our personal stories are not as life threatening as many of the pet owners who sent us letters, but they illustrate our commitment to natural healing and preventive medicine.

→*"My cat Misty was eight years old and although full grown and seemingly healthy, she only weighed four pounds. When I wrote our first pet book, "Are You Poisoning Your Pets?," I took my own advice and started feeding Misty premium cat food and supplements. I added minerals to her water and got rid of her toxic chemical flea collar, preferring to give her nutritional yeast and aged garlic extract supplements as flea prevention. She is now ten, and weighs eight pounds and has not had the sniffles, nor any fleas in two years.*
*Recently, she was bitten. I knew she had a abscess beneath the skin and called the vet to ask what his procedure was. For lots of money, he would lance the wound, put a drain in and give her antibiotics. For free, I applied a hot compress of sea salt and water every few hours until the abscess opened up (24 hours). I gave her echinacea herbal drops diluted in water, with a syringe directly into*

her mouth, fed her a complex mineral, enzyme, vitamin, essential fatty acid and sea vegetable supplement, and mineral water every four hours. Once opened, the wound was treated with liquid aged garlic extract directly into the wound and orally. I continued the supplements for ten days. The wound was completely drained within four days and healed nicely. Once drained and closed, I applied calendula ointment to the wound. She completely recovered using old fashioned home remedies and I saved lots of money!"
-Nina Anderson

→"I have two dogs, a seven-year old greyhound, and a fourteen-year-old Brittany Spaniel. The Brittany had a grand mal seizure (epileptic) a year ago and was near death. I started her on liquid crystalloid trace minerals (electrolyte form) as soon as she stopped shaking. Within one hour, she settled down and fell asleep. I have continued giving her various supplements, containing minerals, vitamins, greens, garlic, sea vegetables and essential fatty acids. I add enzymes to every meal I serve my dogs and feed them only premium dog food or free-range meat scraps. I have found that supplementing her with minerals, nutritional yeast, flax seed and lecithin has helped her retain her coordination and she has not lost any brain function. The garlic seems to help with her arthritis as I found this herb has excellent healing properties for joints. This regime also prevents flea infestations which I'm sure she appreciates. Although she has lost some of her vim and vigor, I am thankful that she is still with me and not in pain."
-Dr. Howard Peiper

→"About two years ago, we were unfortunately faced with our first feather plucking experience. We were caught by surprise when one of our hens, Bronze-Winged Pionus began plucking herself shortly after her babies were removed. I understood her distress when she found her babies gone, but I didn't expect it to develop into a plucking problem! I felt so bad, it was her first year as a breeder at three years of age. After waiting a few months of hoping she'd "get over it" (she didn't), we attempted to pamper her a little bit. She seemed to enjoy the attention we gave her and she became very animated. When we brought her to her mate, she was very happy to see him and they cuddled a lot. She did, however, continue to pick *herself (her chest, abdomen, back, and under wing areas). She was not a pretty sight!*

*After considerable thought about what approach to take next, we decided we would try a calmative herbal formula (valerian/passionflower). Improvement was observed over a two week period. She now has only a few missing feathers and we've caught her picking as soon as something stresses her. We treat her with the calming herbs for two weeks at a time and then stop. It seems some birds become more agitated from change than others. This hen is obviously just more sensitive to changes and disturbances in her environment than our other breeding hens. We are happy that we have a natural remedy for this bird on the occasion that she experiences a stressful event."*

-Alicia McWatters, M.S.

# TABLE OF CONTENTS

# CHAPTER 1. BASIC HEALTH FOR ALL ANIMALS

Household pets die younger now than ever before. Statistics show that the normal lifespan for the average pet dog or cat in the United States, has decreased by approximately eighteen percent in the last forty years. The problem is that our pets are becoming nutritionally deficient, due to the fact that most commercial pet foods lack sufficient minerals, enzymes, and proper nutrients. Commercial grade pet foods may contain harmful additives and processed grains, instead of high quality proteins. These foods weaken the immune system, providing the environment for disease to gain a foothold..

Improving your pet's health is relatively simple. In this book you will learn abouth the importance of minerals, enzymes and essential fatty acids, and the part they play in prolonging  the life of your pet. Some animals are born with deficiencies of these important elements. This is often the result of a malnourished mother. Unfortunately, if the problem is not corrected in the present generation, each subsequent generation inherits a constitution weaker than the one before. A great example of this, is a story you may be familiar with.

→ *Dr. Francis Pottenger studied six hundred cats in the 1930's. He fed these animals good quality beef, until the depression restricted his budget. Half of the cats were put on processed food. Although Dr. Pottenger did not plan to study the effects of this dietary change, he noted that the health of the animals in each group was markedly different. After three generations, the cats fed processed foods developed degenerative diseases such as arthritis, in what would be their teen-age years. He deduced that this occurred because the food was enzyme deficient and the body had to work harder to digest the meals. As each animal became deficient, they had less enzymes to pass along to their offspring. Thus, the domino effect compromised the health of the newer generations.*

Having a good constitution is a major factor in our animal's ability to defend itself against disease. It is wise to prevent disease before it begins, and even an inherently weak constitution my be strengthened through gentle loving care and simple measures that enhance the immune system. This chapter will describe the basics needed by all animals (and humans), which keep their bodies functioning properly.

The basics include minerals and enzymes in the proper amounts from reliable sources. Without them our pets (and their owners) would die. Minerals that used to come to us in perfect balance through our food and drinking water, now are missing or are delivered in a form that cannot be assimilated by the body. This is due to the natural world being altered by modern farming methods, acid rain and other types of pollution. Minerals and enzymes found in complete premium foods can shore-up the old' immune factory and keep those trips to the vet minimal.

→*"We had Emma the __cat__, who was sixteen years old and had substantial kidney damage. The owner contacted me because the cat was dying, <u>literally</u>. They took her to the vet, and she was diagnosed as having __complete renal failure__ and had a hyper thyroid problem. The owner asked if there was anything we could do. They were just watching her slip away day-by-day. She wasn't eating at all. Through kinesiology testing, I found that Emma could handle PHD and would benefit from this premium food. The owner gave her this food along with herbs and vitamins I suggested.*

*Throughout the next week, I received notes and phone messages from Emma's owner telling me that Emma was no longer seeking out dark places and was no longer screaming out in pain. Emma is now back among the living! When we were doing a shoot for one of my videos, Emma was just vibrant. Her skin and coat looked good, her eyes were sparkling, she was purring, you could pat her and touch her anywhere and her weight was back to normal."*
-April Frost, Hearthside Animal Center, New Hampshire


• **MINERALS**

On March 12, 1996, the New York Times reported that wild moose ingested excess concentrations of molybdenum from grazing on pastures where lime was spread to counteract the effects of acidification from rainfall. Excessive molybdenum created a copper deficiency, causing a toxic imbalance in the liver. This copper deficiency caused hundreds of moose to become emaciated. Their hair became discolored, and they suffered from osteoporosis, ulcers, diarrhea, convulsions, blindness and sudden heart failure. If mineral upset can have this disastrous effect in the wild, what are we doing to create similar imbalances in our pets?

Our favorite TV moose who appears in the opening credits of "Northern Exposure" also met his demise because of a mineral (cobalt and copper) deficiency in his diet. Normally moose in the wild live to be sixteen, but fed in captivity by humans, life expectancy is only six or seven years. This may in part be due to a mineral deficiency or imbalance, created by inferior food products and polluted drinking water.

## MINERAL DEFICIENCIES.

We must supplement our pet's diets (and our diets), with useable (by the body) minerals and electrolytes, or face a host of ailments. Mineral deficiencies may appear in pets as sickness or allergy. Lack of zinc for instance, can cause vomiting, conjunctivitis, debility, and retarded growth in cats. Proper levels of zinc give skin and coat protection. Zinc also protects molecules and tissues against free radicals thereby representing an essential component of antioxidant enzymes. Zinc is required for the activity of over 100 different kinds of enzymes in animal health. Calcium deficiencies in dogs result in osteoporosis, hip dysplasia, gum erosion and teeth loss, easily broken bones, and reproductive failures. In cats, symptoms are nervousness, lameness, thin bones and unfriendly behavior.

Copper deficiencies present symptoms such as loss of hair pigmentation and bone abnormalities. Low potassium contributes to muscle weakness, poor growth, listlessness, irregular heartbeat and lesions in the kidneys. Manganese deficiencies can contribute to reproductive dysfunction, weak tendons and ligaments, impaired bone formation, anemia, neuro-muscular dysfunctions, and glandular swelling.

A similar unbalancing of minerals can occur with excessive intake of single vitamins, either by producing a deficiency or increasing the retention of a particular mineral. A high intake of vitamin C decreases copper's absorption and will contribute to a deficiency. Too much zinc can unbalance copper and iron levels in the body. Iron deficiencies can cause anemic conditions, weakness and fatigue.

Excess calcium, sometimes used for breeding and lactating females, can cause kidney failure and stones, as well as contributing to skeletal abnormalities and poor growth. In order to have the calcium absorbed, vitamin D, boron and magnesium must be present. Calcium balanced with magnesium may actually *guard* against stones forming. The effect of calcium-magnesium imbalance has been seen in dairy cattle for years. A condition known as grass staggers exhibits symptoms such as unsteady gait, muscular twitching and uncontrollable flicking of their tail. Without enough magnesium to counterbalance the stimulating effect of calcium, muscles stiffen up or contract at will. The result may be cramps, irritability, twitching or even tremors. Drugs may deplete minerals, by increasing their excretion or interfering with mineral imbalance. All minerals must work together in the proper amounts. To maintain the delicate balance, it is therefore wise to administer any singular mineral supplements without proper guidance.

Each animal is an individual and before you start helping them, you should know where they stand. By performing a "hairpendectomy" (taking a snip of their coat), a tissue mineral analysis can be done by a laboratory. These reports give you information about nutrient mineral levels, toxic metal levels (aluminum, lead, cadmium, mercury), and in some cases, dietary and supplement suggestions. One such laboratory BIO-SPECTRUM ANALYSIS, INC., is listed in the resource directory. Once you have determined what your pet needs you can consult with professionals to develop a proper supplementation program. Please don't "shoot in the dark" by thinking you know what's best without proper analysis!

The following list depicts the function of certain minerals.
•**Calcium:** Bone formation, muscle contraction, metabolism, blood clotting, bone strength.
•**Chloride:** Kidney function, Fluid and acid/alkaline balance.
•**Chromium:** Guards against cardiovascular disease.

4

•**Copper:** Enables incorporation of iron into hemoglobin. Bone & cartilage formation.
•**Fluorine:** Important in bone and teeth development.
•**Iodine:** Constituent of thyroxin for thyroid function, control of metabolism, growth and reproduction.
•**Iron:** Constituent of hemoglobin. Cell metabolism.
•**Magnesium:** Inter-related to calcium and phosphorus for development of bones. Assists metabolism, protein synthesis, nerve excitability and energy production on a cellular level.
•**Manganese:** Assists metabolism of carbohydrates, protein and fats. Calcium and phosphorus utilization, bone development, reproduction and fertility.
•**Pantothenic Acid** is necessary for iron to be incorporated into hemoglobin.
•**Phosphorus:** Assists with metabolism and bone growth.
•**Potassium:** Inter-related to sodium in nerve and muscular function. Balances fluid and cellular metabolism.
•**Selenium:** Inter-related with vitamin E as an antioxidant. Contained in enzyme glutathionine peroxidase which protects muscle membranes.
•**Sulfur:** Amino acids methionine and cystine.
•**Zinc:** Assists metabolism, forms cartilage and hoof. Maintains hair, skin health.

MINERALS FROM DRINKING WATER.
    Bioavailable minerals are in scare supply today in our drinking water. This deficiency is discussed in detail in *WATER in CHAPTER 1*. We suggest using only filtered or bottled water with added electrolyte trace minerals, as an alternative to the potentially hazardous drinking water coming from your tap.

MINERALS FROM VEGETABLE SOURCES.
    If you think you can feed your animals mineral-rich vegetables, think again! Obtaining minerals from vegetable sources is becoming more difficult each year due to non-organic farming methods and acid rain which lowers the pH of the soil. Starved for trace-minerals, plants now take up toxic pesticides, fertilizers and 'bad' minerals. One such mineral aluminum, has caused cats to suffer from a lack of coordination, rabbits to develop memory problems, and birds to lay

eggs with fragile shells. Food processing further depletes the needed micronutrients in our food. Symptoms of deficiencies include coat, skin, and allergy problems, breeding and growth difficulties, weakened immune systems and a general lack of thriftiness. Giving your animal premium pet foods or supplements are necessary to correct any deficiencies.

## MINERAL BALANCE AND SUPPLEMENTATION.

Although many minerals supplements are balanced and safe, they are not all alike in their ability to be utilized by the body. Though a supplement may contain a dozen different minerals, the question is...in what form are those minerals being offered? Colloidal minerals are larger and are less likely to be completely absorbed. Chelated food source minerals (bound with an amino acid) are smaller and therefore better absorbed by the body. Ionic minerals are smaller yet. Crystalloid minerals are the smallest and more likely to be one hundred percent absorbed. A crystalloid is a substance, like a crystal, which forms a true solution and can pass through a living membrane. Crystalloid minerals, when they are electrically charged and found in solution, contain electrolytes (electrical charge necessary for life).

The safest and best way to help your pet is to add a complete mineral supplement to its diet. These should include the trace-minerals such as organic copper, zinc, chromium, selenium, and iodine, micronutrients, plus certain macro-minerals (those needed in large amounts) form the electrolytes which provide the body with vital electrical energy needed to carry out all functions. Liquid products are convenient as they can be dribbled into purified water and given to all types of animals and birds. Supplements can be also be offered in pill form, or as powdered nutrients to mix with food. What follows are two personal accounts of pet owners who gave trace mineral supplements to their animals and experienced great results.

→*"I have a seven year old **cat** by the name of Chancy. She was a show cat for many years and was given to me by the old owner who raised Persians. While I was on vacation, I gave her to a family member to take care of. When I returned we found that Chancy had developed a **bladder infection**. The vet bill came to over $600. and*

6

*although she made progress, the condition returned a few weeks later.*

*When I again contacted the vet, he suggested additional treatment. I could not afford to spend another $600., so I asked the woman who had initially given us the cat, if she had an alternative solution. She suggested that I put Chancy on a liquid mineral supplement called Pet-Lyte. The next morning I put seven drops in Chancy's water and continued in this manner for the next few days. Soon after, I began to notice a change in her personality. She became playful and lively like she had been as a kitten. Ever since then, a day has not passed that I have not given her the mineral supplement. Her infection went away and we have never had a problem since."*

-Lisa LeFebvre, Florida


→*"Three months ago, I purchased a* **mustang mare** *who was in hideous shape. She was about sixty pounds* **underweight,** *and had a* **scruffy winter coat** *about one inch long. Her* **eyes were dull** *and, while she had great bone, she gave a general impression of listlessness. On a whim (really, I never impulse buy at the feed store), I picked up a trial bucket of Source micronutrients and started adding it to the mare's diet. To be fair, let me also add that I was giving her Select NuImage, MSM and probiotics.*

*Three months later, this mare is not recognizable as the same animal I hauled here. Gone is the shaggy coat and in its place is this amazing glassy sheen. In the places on her belly where she is still shedding her dull fuzz, it is remarkable to see the contrast of old and new coat. Her general "flesh" has been compared to a twenty thousand dollar Quarter Horse.*

*Best of all, there is a sparkle in her eye that wasn't there before. She has the stamina to take ten hour rides and seems to be able to sustain her weight on a couple of flakes of grass hay daily. Don't know what affected the change in her most, but I am in the process of isolating the nutrients to see if I can tell. I'll tell you this, Source is the only supplement that was new to my horsekeeping regime and I have never seen shine on a horse of mine like I've seen on this mare."*

-Bonnie Jackson, Oasis Ranch

## • ENZYMES

A body cannot make its own minerals, but it does have the power to make enzymes. They are activated, energized protein molecules; and can be thought of as the construction workers in the body, that build the structure and keep it repaired. There are three primary groups of enzymes: <u>metabolic enzymes</u> that catalyze various chemical reactions within the cells such as detoxification and energy production; <u>digestive enzymes</u> that are secreted along the gastrointestinal tract to break down food allowing nutrient absorption; and <u>antioxidant enzymes</u> which assist in fighting free-radicals and virus'.

Unfortunately, a body can only call upon its enzyme reserves once in a while without overworking the pancreas. Enzymes that are used up in the digestion of food, cause the enzyme storage banks to become depleted. Raw food contains its own enzymes necessary for digestion. When pets chew either raw food or prey, enzymes from that food are activated. After this initial pre-digestion, the food moves to the upper stomach where it continues to break down remaining in this location for an hour before gastric secretions move in. At this point the enzymatic action is disabled by the acids and doesn't kick in again until the food reaches the small intestine where pH is more akaline. Every raw food contains exactly the right amount and types of enzymes to digest that particular food. Cooked food contains no live enzymes. It is therefore a problem to feed pets cooked and processed food day in and day out.

If not enough enzymes are produced, then the food won't digest properly and not only could your pet get a stomach ache, but other effects of maldigestion could appear in the form of 'food allergies, The pancreas can produce digestive enzymes to digest the cooked food, although it was not designed to work overtime. Eventually the pancreas loses the ability to make enzymes, and degenerative disease sets in as depicted by the following story..

→ *"We discovered our **dog**, Chief had **lymph cancer** last fall. Having lost a dog to this same thing a number of years ago, we knew or thought we knew the horrible outcome. However, our veterinarian suggested an extensive chemotherapy treatment which included asparaginase vincristine, cytoxin and other chemotherapy* *drugs. He started his treatments in November. When Chief was three weeks into the treatment he was extremely sore. He was so bad that he could not get up without crying and needed help getting up. It was at this time, Dr. Peterson gave us a small bottle of Prozyme, remarking at the time that he really did not know what it did, but it seemed to help.*

*We started giving him the enzymes along with his regular dog food and a special "chicken stew" we had started feeding him prior to the chemotherapy treatments. Not only were we amazed, but extremely happy when we noticed a few days later he was getting up by himself with only an occasional whimper. He also was moving better when we took him for his morning and evening walks. Not that he needed any complications, but arthritis had begun to be noticed last summer.*

*Chief is now in his final week of treatment, a five day series of intravenous antibiotics. He acts like there had never been anything wrong with him. Anyone not seeing him when he was so excessively stiff and sore, would not believe he had been in that condition seeing him now. In fact, a friend of ours who had seen him when he was so bad, could not believe the remarkable change.*

*Another item of note, prior to the start of his chemotherapy, Chief had lost approximately 15 pounds. He was normally a lean, trim 100 pounds, being taller and longer than the standard German Shepherd, so at 85 pounds he looked skinny. His weight gain started in December right in the middle of chemotherapy treatments. From what we understand about that type of treatment, this is not the normal occurrence. Needless to say, his weight gain did not hurt our feelings whatsoever.*

*We learned that Prozyme would help retard hair loss. It certainly did that. The only hair loss Chief suffered was his whiskers, the longer hairs above the eyes and a couple of thin spots above one eye. The whiskers and longer hairs above the eyes are growing back. At present they are approximately half their normal length and the thin spots are filling in as well.*

*We certainly wish we had known of the benefits of enzymes in the past. We most likely would have had some of our dogs and cats that have died, with us longer than they were."*
-Lee & Sharon, Spokane, WA

Enzymes can't work alone and most require the presence of vitamins and minerals, known as co-enzymes, in order to do their work. Co-enzymes cannot be made by the body. For example, vitamins A, D, E, and K require fat for absorption and in order to be broken down, they need the enzyme, lipase. If it is deficient, fat will not be digested and absorbed, and the vitamins will not be released. Water soluble vitamin B's and C, also help enzymes do their job. Vitamin C is necessary for the enzyme that helps make collagen, a major component of skin. Minerals and electrolytes are necessary because they are part of the enzyme structure. So you see, that if enzymes are not present, the vitamins and minerals have no reason to be in the body.

There are no synthetic enzymes. Only living matter can produce them and because plant enzymes work in a wider range of pH found in the digestive tract, they are better all around enzymes than animal based types. Supplements of plant enzymes help food to be assimilated in order to repair organs, glands, bones, muscles and nerves. Any excess is stored in the liver and the muscles. Like any addition to the body, tread lightly when first adding enzymes to your pet's diet.

## • HEALING FATS

It has been thought that fat people and fat pets need to go on low fat diets. There are even low fat pet foods, but what we tend to overlook is the importance fats have in our bodies. It is not fat that that throws our bodies out of balance, but the type of fat that we eat. Unhealthy fats add cholesterol and excess weight. Good fats help us live longer and include the Omega 3 (alpha linolenic) and Omega 6 (linoleic) essential fatty acids (EFA's). Without adequate stores of them, our cellular neurotransmitters break down and send erroneous signals throughout the body. Essentially, we malfunction. EFA's are not manufactured by the body (in humans or animals), therefore we must depend on food to supply these nutrients to our bodies.

→*"My **dog**, Nikki's was diagnosed with **pancreatitis**. The vet was saying how bad she was and nothing could be used to control her pain and symptoms because she was highly sensitive to all medications. We were afraid that putting her down would soon be* *our only option. I was scared and extremely upset to say the least! I searched out every book store I could find in southern California to find the older herbal and Chinese medicinal remedy books. In them I found specific references to symptoms which resembled Nikki's and the use of olive oil and alfalfa that applied to cases close to hers.*

*I put her on alfalfa and olive oil daily and continued that for the rest of her life. The recommendations in those books turned the situation around and gave her the relief she needed to help her system recover to a point where we could mostly control her bouts of pain and illness. The vet was quite surprised with what I was doing and the positive results we obtained."*

-Dawn Hoffman, Ohio

Dogs, cats and horses need less oil than humans, but must depend on us to feed them essential fatty acid fortified food. Many pet food manufacturers use too few EFA's in their recipes. Oils will become rancid if exposed to oxygen, therefore manufacturers are reluctant to put too many in their cans. The other choice they have, is to add refined (heated), non-organic high EFA oils such as corn. Heat processing limits the potential for rancidity, but also kills most of the complementary nutrients in the oils.

Many pet foods only contain one type of EFA causing an imbalance and creating further deficiencies. For instance, if Omega 6 is not balanced by Omega 3, the arachidonic acid in the Omega 6 can get out of hand. Normally required for cellular growth, if left unchecked, this can create an overabundance of growth cells. If these cells are cancerous, then the situation could be life threatening. (Recent studies have shown that garlic can have a tempering effect on this cellular overgrowth caused by this type of EFA imbalance.)

DIFFERENT STROKES FOR DIFFERENT FOLKS.

The EFA balance in oils given to dogs, cats, horses and humans needs to be different for each. Horses natural diet is rich in Omega 3, therefore feed with corn oil added (mostly Omega 6), is an unhealthy choice. Essential fatty acids are bioavailable to the body when in the complement of 'minor' nutrients such as phytosterols, lecithin, vitamin E, and carotene The refining and heat extraction methods normally used, depletes the oils of these nutrients. Cold

11

extraction methods are far superior and leave most oils as nature had intended. Flax oil (Omega 3), sunflower and sesame seed oil (Omega 6) are a good combination.

Oil supplements must be chosen carefully. Flax meal containing fiber, amino acids, and other nutrients for metabolism is a good choice and easy to mix into food. Bottled oils are excellent if they are cold extracted, organic, are in a dark bottle and have been kept away from light, which can promote rancidity once the bottle is opened. Flax oil, although wonderful for humans, can cause oxidative damage to tissues in cats and dogs, if given without the complementary 'minor' nutrients mentioned above.

GETTING OILS INTO THE BODY.

Essential fatty acids must be synthesized in the body; this requires Biotin, an essential B vitamin that works as a nutritional enzyme for the synthesis of fatty acids. Biotin also helps metabolize carbohydrates and proteins, maximizing the nutritional value of your pet's diet. Certain common practices destroy this vitamin. Chlorinated water coming from your tap inactivates biotin. which is also destroyed by rancidity from fat and meat by-products (a common hazard of storing opened cans of food for a period of time.) Avidin, a substance found in raw egg whites, also destroys biotin. Pet foods containing egg products may contain avidin. Antibiotics and sulfonamides may decrease the natural intestinal synthesis of biotin, therefore pets on these medications should definitely be given biotin and vitamin E supplements. Biotin supplements should also be included in your pet's food to prevent the loss of bioavailability of essential fatty acids.

The enzyme lipase also must be present to break down fats. If your pet's levels of enzymes are depleted due to a constant cooked food diet, the essential fatty acids and other fats will not be digested. Plant enzyme supplements should be added to your animal's cooked food diet for this reason among others stated in the section on Enzymes.

HEALTH BENEFITS OF EFA's.

Given the proper balance of essential fatty acids, you will soon notice your pet's coat becoming thick and shiny. EFA's are extremely beneficial to skin and hair and can appear as a miracle

12

cure. Dry flaky skin, increased cutaneous infections and hair loss in animals, is a good indication of EFA deficiencies. Many natural supplements found in the marketplace today, contain the proper complement of EFA's along with the 27 essential nutrients required for oil metabolism. The results produced include ceasing of excessive shedding, disappearance of feline acne and hair balls, improvement of doggy odors, drippy eyes and tear stained faces, elimination of dry skin, eczema, hot spots and oily skin, re-growth of hair, increased energy levels, reduction in symptoms of hip dysplasia, digestive problems lessened and greater performance and stamina. The following letter illustrates the success of one of these multi-nutrient supplements containing EFA's.

→*"I have owned **dogs** for twenty-five years and have been active in hunting, obedience, confirmation and agility. A year ago, we fenced in a new section of our property next to the woods and fields. The dogs were busy investigating, eating grass, digging holes and eating dirt. I am employed by a local animal hospital and test my dogs for parasites yearly. The results have always been negative.*

*Their last stool exam showed eggs unlike anything I'd ever seen before. The hospital doctors could not confirm what they were and so a sample was sent to the lab for analysis. Results showed hooks, coccidia and round worms in all three of my dogs. None of them had ever had any **parasites** before. The interesting point was that none of these eggs looked normal and were unidentifiable by us at the hospital. Why? They appeared much smaller and incompletely formed. Also, none of my dogs showed any ill health. All had normal stools and were in excellent coat, high energy, normal appetites, etc.*

*We had been using Nupro supplement for several months and the dogs were thriving on it. I feel very strongly that Nupro's ingredients interfered with the development of these parasites and prevented serious illness as a result. Had I been feeding Nupro before they had a six month start in the dirt, perhaps they would not have developed parasites at all."*
-Cheryl Whitmore, New Jersey

→*"Our seventeen-plus year old Siamese **cat**, Pyewacket, was as one neighbor kindly put it, "**on her last legs.**" The veterinarian said she*

*had outlived her organs. My father assumed she'd be gone by Labor Day. My sister recommended I give her a supplement, Missing Link. I did and within a week, Pyewacket's appetite was amazingly improved and she was drinking water regularly again. Her legs are stronger and she jumps to her favorite sofa inside and her perch on the table outside. Her voice is stronger (the only improvement we could have done without as she tends to exercise it in the middle of the night), and she has rejoined her friends in play. This supplement rich in essential fatty acids, is the only new addition to her regime and it sure has improved the quality of her life."*
-Muff Singer, California

## • WATER

You may wonder why we discuss water as an essential element that is in short supply in the body. Pets, especially indoor pets, depend on their owners to provide them with enough water for optimum health. This sounds simple, but how often do our hectic lives get in the way of remembering to fill their water dish, or at least checking it several times a day to see if it's empty. Animals being fed dry food may suffer from dehydration as dry food contains only twelve percent moisture, as opposed to about an eighty percent moisture content that would be found in the wild or in canned food.

Not only should pet owners be conscious of providing ample water for their pet, but they should determine if the water is pure. Acid rain, pesticides, agricultural runoff, and industrial pollution tend to change the constitution of our water sources, not only making it hazardous to drink, but mixing many bad minerals (lead, mercury, cadmium) with the good. Too bad for the wild animals, but you give your pet tap water which has to be better.....right?

Wrong! Tap water has been chlorinate, fluoridated, and treated which removes many mineral and because it may pick up bacteria on its way to your sink, it may not be healthy to drink. Well water is probably better, but then again environmental pollution or agricultural runoff could be sending hazardous water to your well. Your solution may include drinking bottled water or filtered water, but do you give it to your pets, or are they still relegated to tap water?

HOW TO CLEAN YOUR WATER.

Several methods of home treatment are available. Whole house filters can be installed, or you can use counter-top or under the sink, point of use filters on your faucet. Carbon, KDF and other types of filters are available to remove many contaminants, although Reverse Osmosis units will take out 98% of the dissolved solids and Distillation will remove 100%. What ever method you decide upon, please make sure your pet receives the same pure water as you drink. Since reverse osmosis or distillation removes many of the minerals, it is important to add a liquid mineral supplement with electrolytes, to your water or face many of the diseases caused by deficiencies. The two most important health devices you should invest in, are a water filtration system and an air purification device.

## • CLEAN AIR

Indoor pets have a distinctive disadvantage over outdoor animals. They depend on humans to provide them with fresh air to breathe. That could be a big mistake, as most pet owners are not even aware of the need for clean air in their homes. Many people and pets too, suffer from allergies. Many of these come from airborne pathogens, mold, dust and outgassing chemical fumes from carpets, cleaners, stain resistant fabrics and other decorating materials which you may not have know are even hazardous. In some cases, our homes become toxic gas chambers for the animals we love. Outdoor pets may be at risk if you live in an area of high air pollution, but statistics show that indoor air, potentially can be dirtier than outside city air.

HOW TO CLEAN YOUR AIR.

The solution is simple. Install one of the many types of air cleaners or air purifiers being sold today. Ozone generating machines are effective against dust, mold, bacteria, airborne pathogens and chemicals. If these units contain an ionizer, they create an atmosphere similar to the calming effect noticed after a thundershower passes. This negative ionization of the air tends to calm pets, especially birds. The ozone also tends to kill certain bacteria that may cause skin reactions and make animals scratch or birds peck their feathers. Electronic air filters are effective against

15

dust and also animal dander, mold fragments and odors. High efficiency particulate arrestor (HEPA) filters and carbon filters have been combined in many units and are also extremely effective at keeping the air indoors, fresh and clean. Which ever type of unit you decide is best, for your pet's sake, make this purchase a priority.

Air exchange is also important. Heat recovery ventilators and air exchangers are offered in homes under construction, but if you have a well insulated home with no mechanical means of getting the air in, then open a window from time to time. The fresh air is definitely worth the price you pay for a little heat loss.

→ *"A friend of mine had a __dog__ boarding kennel which had good ventilation in the summer, but when winter came she had to close the windows. She noticed the animals who were residents of longer than a week, exhibited signs of __depression__ or became __irritable__. She also had a high rate of __watery eyes and sniffles__, even though she kept the place immaculate. She thought the problem might stem from the stuffy air and started investigating air purification systems. She decided upon an Alpine unit which uses ozone to clean the air. This seemed to stop the drippy eyes and sniffles, but she also noticed her animals calmed down and seemed happier.*

*The Alpine representative told her it was probably due to the ion generator that was part of the unit. It seems that in the winter static electricity builds up inside buildings creating positive ions. These have a negative effect on emotions. Once the air purifier started delivering both positive and __negative__ ions, a balance was created and the static electricity diminished along with the depression and anxiety. It also helped her business because the pets went home without the kennel cough or nervous behavior normally associated with a stay in a boarding facility."*
B.R., Massachusetts

## • LIGHT

Outdoor animals don't have the problem of the SAD syndrome (seasonal affective disorder), but indoor pets do. Just like people, light plays an important part in the mood of an animal. Being deprived of natural sunlight, such as we find in many homes and apartments, can affect the health of your dog, cat, ferret or bird.

Horses may be lucky enough to have a sunlit pasture to romp in, but many are cooped up most of the day in dingy barn stalls with very little light at all. And we wonder why they are restless and whinny so much! Lack of sunlight can cause functional disorders of the nervous system, a vitamin D deficiency, a weakening of the body's defenses and an aggravation of chronic diseases.

Light is a nutrient, similar to all the other nutrients we take in through food, and we need the full range of natural daylight, This is a fact long since proven by science. If you have enough sunny windows, dogs and cats will find their way to "light", but caged pets or animals in stalls don't have the luxury of finding their own source of vitamin D. Move cages to the sunny area and try to arrange for horses to be outside during the day. If this is not possible, then you should supplement your indoor environmental light with full spectrum light bulbs which mimic sunlight. Available for many years as 'grow' lights for plants, these bulbs come in a variety of shapes and sizes to fit your lighting fixture.

Horse breeders who have begun to use full spectrum lights in their barns, have seen mares experience easier foaling. Radiation shielded full-spectrum light sources have also seemed to help minimize joint pain and relieve respiratory problems. Bird breeders find that full spectrum lighting has a calming effect on their birds, their eggs appear stronger and fertility rates are higher. These benefits are in addition to the personality changes seen by animals, where natural or simulated sunlight creates happier well adjusted pets.

*photo by Neil Shively*

## • NATURAL REMEDIES

This book is about preventive measures you can take to keep your pet in tip top shape. In this chapter we will describe some of the common 'home' remedies that you can investigate. We still advise that you receive a proper diagnosis and recommendation from an allopathic or holistic veterinarian, before proceeding with any natural medications.

HERBS.

Herbs have been used for centuries for healing and illness prevention. Domestic and wild animals still go to plants naturally when they need medication or internal cleansing. Herbs are natural sources of vitamins, antioxidants, minerals, enzymes, amino acids, proteins, sugars, carbohydrates, chlorophyll, trace elements and essential fatty acids. They are balanced and therefore easily assimilated by the body. Herbs work in partnership with the body and help the body to heal itself. Herbs assist in the healing process by helping the body to eliminate toxins, thus reducing symptoms. They may stimulate physiological processes like emptying of the bowels or bladder or act as a liver cleanse, and can serve as immune system builders.

→"I am Pervis the __Cat__ and I'm five years old. When I was one and a half years old, the vet told my owner, Mike, the I'd come down with __feline infectious peritonitis (FIP)__. I had constant diarrhea and vomiting and was down to four pounds. The vet suggested I be put to sleep. (I thought I was too young to die!)

My owner thought there must be an answer so he tried 5cc of liquid Kyolic aged garlic extract every two hours five times a day. In four weeks I'd gained my weight back and was playing with the other cats. Best of all, none of my friends contracted FIP. After six weeks, Mike took me back to the vet and was he amazed. He had never seen or heard of any cat that had survived FIP. I'm happy to say, I'm still in perfect health."
-Pervis the Cat, California

Chinese herbs are normally *custom-tailored* to the individual needs of the patient. Chinese herbs have to be adapted to each condition for pets in regards to dosage and liver function. Herb-Cetera, with help from Dr. Arthur Shattuck, master herbalist, created Pet Therapy to treat animals by balancing their bodies. If an animal's disharmony is too hot, they use cooling herbs; too cool, heating herbs. If there is pain or "stagnation of Qi" (the energy or life force that circulates through a body), they seek herbs that disperse that stagnation thereby alleviating the pain. Since they are not able to get exact information from the animals on how they feel, they carefully supervise and observe the patient and monitor the effects of the herbs administered to assure success. There are little or no side effects when a balanced formula is administered. Chinese herbs are effective for chronic conditions such as arthritis, and undefinable conditions like anxiety. They are normally not effective for acute conditions needing immediate treatment such as shock.

→*"Mishu, a __cat__, had a history of __urinary crystals__, that always resulted in pain, bleeding and an eventual trip to the vet to resolve the problem. Not only was the owner uncomfortable because of the vet bill, but poor Mishu was constantly in pain that he experienced at least once a year. His owner changed Mishu's diet as was prescribed by the vet, but his condition only improved while using Crystal Clear. This herbal formula uses herbs that break down the stones and help wash out the fine sandy gravel that is found in the urinary tract. It is a cooling formula that promotes the flow of water so the "heat" of the infection and stones are balanced and dispersed. Since using Crystal Clear, Mishu has been free of urinary tract crystals for over three years with no adverse effects."*
-Laura Mignosa, Connecticut

"Western" herbology is more available *over-the-counter*, and familiarization with each plant's healing properties is essential. Any herb used as a medicinal should be recommended by a skilled herbal practitioner to avoid harmful dosages or inaccurate diagnosis. Some herbs are great for dogs, but not healthy for cats. For instance, Willowbark is known to be toxic to felines. Herbal formulas have been know to successfully treat arthritis, hip dysplasia, skin problems, hair loss, vomiting, respiratory infections, bladder and kidney disorders, and a host of other maladies. As a reference we will list some common herbs that you may consider using. As with any illness, we recommend that you consult a veterinarian or alternative practitioner. The following report from Aequus Veterinary Service outlines treatment with herbs.

→*CASE 3: 13 year old Standard __Poodle__.*
*Complaint: __Weight loss__, __slight ataxia in hindquarters__, __lethargy__, sudden __aged appearance__ and possible __mental deterioration__*

*(delayed response to stimuli, confusion with doors and corners of rooms).*

*Exam: Dog was fairly bright and alert, but there appeared to be hearing loss as the dog did not seem to respond to low frequency voices or calls. The dog was approximately five to ten percent below ideal body weight. Mild ataxia was present in hind legs with marked wear of dorsal surface of hind nail. There was moderate atrophy of both hamstring muscle groups. Mental attitude was one of anxiety and timidity.*

*Treatment: The dog was chiropractically adjusted. Dietary recommendations were made to remove the dog from processed dry food and put on partially cooked meatloaf diets (Pitcairn). Pastas, grains and vegetables were recommended as often as dog would eat until weight was closer to ideal. Dog was put on Bach Rescue Remedy and Vetri-Science Cell-Advance 880.*

*Response: Two months post treatment, dog is continuing to show improvement, both physically and mentally. She is no longer acting as timid and subordinate around other dogs and strangers. The owner thinks she can hear better. Appetite has improved and dog is gaining weight. Dog has had Vetri-Science Vetri-Disk, Vetri-Science GlycoFlex 600 and Coyote Springs, Senior Support combination herbs added to the above regimen.*

The following stories illustrate the importance of herbal combinations. Ojibwa Tea was developed by Rene Caisse as a potential cancer cure.

→*"As you know, Rene Caisse worked with small animals while trying to find the proper mixture of herbs for human consumption. Therefore, it's not surprising that many people give the tea to their pets as a general tonic. Such was the case of Tigger, our fourteen year old female **cat**. About a year ago, Tigger started to **lose the fur** on her back and hind quarters. On several occasions, she would walk forward with her front legs, while her rear legs walked in a different direction. We had also noticed, on previous occasions, that she seemed to have a weakness in her rear legs and we took this to be some form of **arthritis**.*

*About six months ago, Tigger was sitting on a chair looking out of the window when we heard a thump and found her lying on the*

20

*carpet unable to get up. We thought she was having a stroke. She stretched out her legs, rolled her eyes and moaned in pain. As this happened in the late evening, nothing could be done about it until the next morning. The cat was somehow able to crawl into a secluded place, where we left her to her fate. During the night we heard another thump and assumed that Tigger had dropped dead.*

*When I got up in the morning prepared to do my duty and bury a dead cat, I had trouble finding her. I finally located her under the bed and still alive, but unable to walk. My wife picked her up and knowing that Tigger's digestive system was still working (she eliminated), my wife decided to give her a drink adding a few drops of OJIBWA TEA to the distilled water. Over the next two months, we gave Tigger the tea every day and that cat completely recovered. All the fur grew back and her coat never looked better! Now, she plays like a kitten again and when she was recently examined by a vet, her heart, teeth, eyes, ears and all her bodily functions were found to be in perfect condition."*

-Dave Moffat, Ontario, Canada


→*"Sam Gutterman, a nine year old miniature apricot **poodle**, seemingly in good health, was stricken with a severe case of **pancreatitis** in the early morning hours of Sunday, October 31, 1993. It wasn't his first attack, but this time threatened to be imminently fatal. Fortunately, his veterinarian, Dr. D. E. Huber, determined that the abscess on Sam's pancreas was the size of a grapefruit. Sam's entire belly isn't the size of a grapefruit so this diagnosis was truly not good news. Dr. Huber immediately put Sam on an I.V. antibiotic and pain medication. After forty-eight hours of observation, it was clear that surgery was necessary.*

*Sam survived his operation, but his little seventeen pound body was working overtime trying to be well. Down deep inside, we all thought we were doomed to lose him. His exertion at just being alive was heartbreaking. Just a few hours after surgery, I started administering OJIBWA EXTRACT, five drops at a time, three times a day with Dr. Huber's approval. He predicted that to shrink an abscess of this size might take six to eight weeks. Three days later, the abscess had shrunk to the size of an orange.*

*We continued to visit Sammy at least three times a day to give him his extract and his progress accelerated with each passing day.*

*Within nine days of the operation, Dr. Huber found Sam sufficiently healthy to discharge him and send him home. An exam two days later showed the abscess to be the size of a walnut. Dr. Huber said that in thirty years of practice, he'd never seen a pup survive as severe a case of pancreatitis as Sam's. The treatment Sam received was standard procedure and consisted of surgery, flushing, drains and antibiotics. In addition to the conventional medicine, Sam received the OJIBWA extract three times a day and continues to receive it twice a day now that he is healthy."*
-The Loving Family of Sam Gutterman

Following, is a partial list of herbs for pets, along with some of their benefits. For a more comprehensive look at herbal healing methods for animals read *The Natural Remedy Book for Dogs & Cats* by Diane Stein, *Your Cat Naturally* by Grace McHattie or the chapter "Alternative Healing Options For Pets" in Linda Rector Page's book, *Healthy Healing.* Again, please consult your holistic veterinarian prior to administering herbs as some may be toxic to specific animal species.

•**Alfalfa** contains every vitamin and mineral. It acts as a blood cleanser and detoxifier and is used for allergies, arthritis, kidney and urinary infections and as a tonic.
•**Aloe Vera** is an excellent colon cleanser and remedy for soothing the stomach, liver, kidneys, spleen and bladder. It contains anti-inflammatory agents and has been called the 'wound hormone." It has the ability to penetrate all seven layers of the skin for maximum healing.
•**Arnica** in herbal tincture or cream form, is useful in pain reduction of sprains and bruises. Can affect sensitive skin if used undiluted.
•**Barberry** is mainly used in the treatment of liver problems. It promotes the flow of bile, stimulates digestion and appetite, and lessens constipation.
•**Bearberry** soothes and tones the lining of the bladder and helps the urinary tract. It is antiseptic and diuretic and helpful for cystitis, bladder stones, incontinence and kidney failure.
•**Black Walnut** is excellent to treat skin conditions. It is useful to expel internal parasites and tapeworms.

•**Boswella** is a potent herb for inflammatory disease such as arthritis. This gummy extract from the Boswella tree is being used on horses and dogs with great success. It acts by mechanism similar to non-steroidal groups of anti-arthritic drugs with a plus being, very few side effects.

•**Buchu** helps in the treatment of cystitis and bladder weakness.

•**Burdock** is useful in treating dry skin, scalp, hair and for eczema. It also has been helpful with rheumatism. Burdock root is alkalizing and soothing to the stomach and intestines.

•**Calendula** or marigold, is used on the skin for fast healing of wounds. It reduces swelling and is regenerating as well as anti-microbial. Caution: Calendula closes the skin rapidly so in the case of abscesses, make sure the wound has drained completely before applying.

•**Cascara Sagrada** is nature's answer to a laxative.

•**Catnip** in addition to being an aphrodisiac for cats, can help with fever, flatulence and digestive pain, soothe nerves and act as a sedative.

•**Cat's Claw (Una de Gato)** active constituents, oindole alkaloids, have been proven to increase the ability of the white blood cells and macrophages to attack and digest abnormal cells, harmful microorganisms and toxic matter. The inner bark contains the medicinal properties. Results with humans include help for tumors, arthritis, allergies, respiratory infections, parasites, intestinal disorders. Similar success can be expected in animals as well. Cat's Claw contains numerous plant substances that have tremendous antioxidant properties more powerful than vitamin E and C. Although this herb is considered non-toxic, recommended dosages for animals should not exceed 50-100 mg. per ten pounds of body weight, without consulting a practitioner.

→*"My main area of interest is in treating cats. I have used Cat's Claw quite a bit and it is a really useful all around treatment for boosting their immune systems, especially during times of illness. The main advantage is that it is so well tolerated by cats who often vomit up other herbal products. For very young kittens, I open the capsules and sprinkle it on their food and rather tan putting them off, they seem to like the taste. When it is time to give them their*

*vaccinations, which compromises the immune system, I add Cat's Claw to their diet for several weeks prior before we visit the vet."*
-Brian Christopher, Maine

•**Cayenne pepper** or Capsicum is described as a blood stimulant as well as an insect repellent if taken internally. It also is useful in treating worms, as an antiseptic, and can improve appetite and ease colic. It has been used to help stop shock and aid in heart seizure.

•**Chamomile** is an antispasmodic, and also is a sedative. It works to reduce stomach pains, colic and earache. Topically, it can draw out skin toxins and help with inflammations. An extract of this herb is commonly used in moisturizers due to the high content of levomenol (an anti-inflammatory agent that is excellent at soothing dry and cracked skin.)

→*"We have several __cats__ and have recently had a problem with Murray, our two year old. He came home one day with a __hole in his leg__. It was incredibly raw. I could easily tell that he was in tremendous pain. The hole was so large that we were sure we would have to take him to the vet for stitches. The only thing that came to mind was that someone must have shot my Murray!*

*My husband had recently purchased a pet spray, Skin-Aide, that included minerals, chamomile, comfrey, burdock root, horsetail and aloe vera. We decided to try this on Murray and were amazed that he sat there during the application (cat's usually panic with sprays). We sprayed it on the raw area several times a day. By the next morning, I was shocked to see how much improvement had occurred. After a few days, the wound was only a shadow of what it had once been. About a month later, my ten year old son David, cut himself and I used the skin spray on him. Within an hour, his injury had already begun to scab over."*
-Theresa Aponte, Florida

•**Comfrey** is a natural soothener, internally and externally. It aids in healing of burns, skin ulcers, cuts, abscesses, insect bites, bruises, boils, sprains, fractures and swelling. Comfrey causes bacteria to multiply so rapidly that it implodes upon itself due to weak cell walls, and then disintegrates, making it an excellent treatment against bacteria.

•**Couchgrass** leaves are eaten by dogs and cats to induce vomiting, or as a laxative. Birds eat the seeds for bladder ailments and constipation. The silica content of Couchgrass helps to strengthen teeth, beaks and claws.

•**Dandelion** is useful in treating liver problems. It has a powerful diuretic effect and because of its cleansing nature can help arthritis and rheumatism. Its bitter taste helps promote digestion and appetite.

•**Dill** improves appetite and digestion and is food for relief of flatulence.

•**Echinacea** is nature's antibiotic and should be used *medicinally*, not on a regular basis. This extract can be painted on ringworm to dry it up. When mixed with Black Walnut extract diluted, can expel worms such as pinworms and tapeworms.

•**Elderberry** is used in the treatment of bruises and sprains. It also works for constipation and catarrhal inflammation of the upper respiratory tract. If taken over a period of time, will help purify the blood.

•**Eucalyptus** is well known for its antiseptic action and for its use in treating respiratory conditions. Historically, as an inhalant, it has been used to treat influenza in horses and distemper in dogs.

•**Garlic** is known as the supreme immunizer antioxidant and helps in preventing fleas, worms, ticks, lice, gastric and skin problems. Animals in the wild periodically seek out areas of garlic. This herb is of value in treating fevers, skin conditions, respiratory tract problems, some gastrointestinal conditions, rheumatism and as a general antiseptic and cleanser. It also helps to restore the gut flora following disturbances and helps the heart by lowering blood pressure.

→*"In our valley, many __dogs__ were dying of acute toxemia from a __parvo epidemic__, a new strain of virus in dogs that causes severe hemorrhagic gastroenteritis and death. The percentage of mortality in these dogs was running very high when treated only with practices employing standard/orthodox therapies. When Kyolic Liquid Aged Garlic Extract was added, along with a total treatment regime, I was able to successfully treat the Parvo Virus, and save many of my parvo dogs. I found that the aged garlic extract is effective against fleas, ticks and other parasites as well as being an excellent supplement for the maintenance and promotion of the* general health of animals. It strengthens their immune systems, helps their bodies to eliminate toxins, invigorates the animals, and improves the quality of their coat.

I advise pet owners to administer Kyolic Liquid in the following dosages: small cats and toy breeds, 1/2 tsp. 3 times per day for 1 week and thereafter 1/2 tsp. once a day; medium sized animals increase to 1 tsp. each dosage and for large animals 1 tbsp."
-Dr. Gloria Dodd, D.V.M., California


→"My little **dog**, Bananas came down with quite a bad case of **kennel cough** recently. I started giving her twice as much Kyolic Aged Garlic Extract as I normally do (twelve drops instead of six). I was all ready to start her on medication (antibiotics and steroids), but the kennel cough went away in twenty four hours. I attribute that to the garlic she had already been getting, plus the increase in the dose. Normally it takes kennel cough at least four or five days to go away
-Claire Ives, Utah


•**Ginger** is a stimulant and can ease stomach and bowel pains. It is good assisting in decongesting nasal passages.

•**Goldenseal** is also an antibiotic, a sulfa equivalent. It can be used with echinacea to dry up ringworm, but it will stain fur.

•**Hawthorn** is one of the best herbs for the heart and for circulation. It also is useful as a heartworm preventive.

•**Horsetail** is a rich source of silica needed to keep the skin moist and elastic. This herb is good to repair scar tissue and eliminate swelling. It imparts strength to nails and luster to the skin and coat.

•**Juniper** is a diuretic and is used in cases of cystitis and urethritis.

•**Licorice** is a good expectorant and used for treating bronchitis and respiratory problems, coughs, catarrhal conditions and even chronic constipation and skin conditions. Because of licorice's glycyrrhizin content it is a good alternative for steroid therapy, used to relieve inflammation without drug side effects. Glycyrrhizin stimulates the adrenals into action while introducing its own anti-inflammatory, antimicrobial, immune-supporting corticosteroid-like reaction to the body.

•**Milk Thistle** has been use for centuries as folk remedies for boils and skin diseases, hepatitis and liver problems, especially those associated with environmental pollution. Since the liver takes the most abuse from the toxic lifestyles we inflict on our pets, the preservative and chemical laden food we give them and the drugs and chemical flea collars, sprays, shampoos we subject them too, they need something to help detoxify their bodies. Milk thistle can assist in the cleansing of these pollutants from their bodies.

•**Mullein** helps relieves congestion.

•**Neem** seeds and leaves have been used to construct a new class of "soft" insecticides that are non-toxic to animals, birds and even beneficial insects. It does not affect the nervous system and is non-toxic if ingested. Topically, it is useful against fungi, allergies and mange, ringworm, eczema, infections and internal parasites. It can protect pets from fleas, ticks and mites without harming the animal. It is also useful as a garden and lawn spay in place of toxic chemicals which will affect pets who play outdoors.

•**Nettles** are known to help rheumatism, arthritis and skin disorders. Also, because of its diuretic effect, it helps cleanse the blood and is indicated in bladder and urinary infections. Historically it has been used as a tonic for the coat, making the hair shine, removing scurf and as a valuable treatment for eczema. Some suggest using it as a treatment for anemia because of its high iron content.

•**Parsley** is a rich source of vitamins B, C, A, potassium and iron, thereby being a good blood strengthener. It also helps with joint stiffness, bad breath, obesity and bladder problems. It can reduce flatulence and increase milk production in nursing bitches.

•**Pau D'arco** provides resistance to various infections as it possesses antibiotic properties.

•**Peppermint** promotes digestion by smoothing muscle tissue of the stomach, and eases gas pains. It also can help with motion sickness. and is known to restore appetites in dogs .

•**Raspberry Leaf** assists whelping by strengthening the pelvic muscles, toning the uterus and reducing the risk of hemorrhage. It helps to bring fluid to the birth canal to help prevent dry painful births.

•**Skullcap** has a reputation as a general tonic for the nervous system. It has long been used in the treatment of epilepsy and rabies. It has a calming effect and is useful in cases of excitability, nervous spasms, fits and paralysis.

•**Slippery elm** is good for very young, old or weak cats and dogs. It coats inflamed tissue internally and is useful for ulcers, constipation, diarrhea, dysentery and colitis. Externally it can be used on wounds, burns, abscesses, insect bites.

•**Southernwood** is a de-wormer for dogs and cats. It also acts as a heartworm preventive for dogs, given every other day from April to October. It makes blood bitter in animals and they become less appealing to mosquitoes.

•**Valerian** works as a sedative and as a calming herb for nervousness and excitability. It acts on the higher nerve centers promoting sleep and in some situations, reducing pain.

•**Yarrow** stops internal bleeding and is good for fevers. It may be helpful for diabetic animals as its chemical makeup is close to insulin. Externally, yarrow is an antiseptic for rashes, wounds, and deep punctures.

•**Yew** is a medicinal herb currently harvested from the bough tips of the Yew tree. It is effective for bursitis, joint problems, arthritis, skin problems such as allergy rashes, big bites, basil cell carcinoma skin cancer. Historically, Native Americans have used the yew for pain, fever, colds, stomach distress, as a diuretic and the alleviate the pain during childbirth.

→*" I've been a guide and outfitter in northwestern Montana for nineteen years and I use **horses** extensively in my operation. Due to the steep rise and ruggedness of the terrain, some of my older horses developed **inflammation problems in their front legs**. Knowing that the Montana Yew tincture had strong anti-inflammatory properties, I began using it on my older horses by putting it in their grain.*

*I found that twenty drops per hundred pounds of body weight was effective in reducing inflammation. During our busy season, daily administrations proved to be a valuable preventative of this condition. I also use the Montana Yew tincture on my older hound dogs who often suffer from arthritic symptoms. I noticed that it relieves their stiffness significantly and increases their energy and stamina. On one occasion, Montana Yew tincture and salve effectively relieved the symptoms of Lupus in a friend's pedigree German Shepherd. "*
-Rus Willis, Montana

•**Yucca** is useful as a laxative, diuretic and antiseptic. It is helpful for ulcers, sore joints and arthritis and as a pain reliever and also an effective anti-virul and anti-fungal agent.

FLOWER REMEDIES.

In the 1930's the noted British physician, Dr. Edward Bach developed the natural healing methods of flower remedies. He believed that the stress, and emotional imbalances were important in creating a healthy body and reducing stress. Flower remedies address every emotional condition and imbalance that can contribute to illness. They address the cause of the problem, not the symptom, and are all natural and safe. These remedies work by addressing emotions only, and do not interfere with any other type of treatment or with any physical functioning. Among the many emotions that flower remedies can help are sadness, rage, nervousness and stress from travel in carriers and crates, on airplanes, cars and trains.

*photo by Neil Shively*

•**Aspen** is used for calming nerves on animals that are easily frightened, especially of the unknown.

•**Cherry Plum** is useful on aggressive animals that appear uncontrollable.

•**Chestnut Bud** targets animals that are difficult to train. It helps correct unhealthy habits and negative behavior.

•**Chicory** can be for an animal that follows you around, is constantly underfoot and becomes extremely upset when left alone. For the jealous pet.

•**Clematis** can be used on lethargic pets.

•**Impatiens** can be used on impatient, fast-paced, irritable animals.

•**Larch** is effective in helping animals that lack self confidence in the pecking order.

•**Mimulus** is for reducing fears of timid animals.

•**Rock Rose** helps animals that panic easily or who have experienced terror.

•**Scleranthus** alleviates car sickness.

•**Star of Bethlehem** works on animals who have been abused or who have lost a loved pet or human companion.

•**Water Violet** is for the animal who tend to be loners (especially cats).

•**Calming Essence** from Ellon includes a wide-range of flower essences that are used for trauma. They can also be used as a calming agent for travel, after surgery or accidents, for panicked animals or anytime stress reduction is needed. Both include Star of Bethlehem, Rock Rose, Clematis, Cherry Plum and Impatiens.

→*"I have been showing __cats__ for many years, and recently noticed that my cats appeared much more __fidgety__ than many of the other cats being shown. It began to concern me, so I spoke to several of the other exhibitors, who suggested that I use Calming Essence flower remedy. It was fantastic. For the first time, my prize show cat sat calmly before, and during the show. She was rewarded with a ribbon at the show. Since then, I have used it with my cats before we leave for the show, when we arrive, and about ten minutes before showing. We've had our best results ever!"*
-M.G., New Mexico

## TACHYONIZED ENERGY.

Tachyon energy, otherwise known as life force energy is not a specific nutrient, yet it has been proven to have an integral part in the healing realm. When it is blocked, our electrical system can short circuit and prevent healing. From experience, we know that we can clear such blocks by using high quality organic foods, natural supplements, essences, and now with the newly developed life force energy antennae.

*photo by Star Dewar*

For the first time in history, we have scientific methods of restructuring certain materials at the sub-molecular level that then become antennae that attract and focus usable biological energy; Tachyon energy. These tools provide the energy needed to begin the balancing process from the inside out. This is not a fanciful theory, but rather a conceptual revelation, taking root worldwide as the rejuvenating benefits of Tachyon energy are demonstrated on a global scale.

→*"Paulette, a friend of mine's thirteen year old __Golden Lab__ was diagnosed with __pancreatic failure__ and given only one week to live. My heart was open as I held my friend in my arms and we both cried. I didn't see Paulette for almost two months and when I did, I couldn't believe my eyes! The dog was perfectly healthy. My friend told me that she had used Tachyon water drops in Paulette's mouth and put large Tachyon cells in her bed as well as a cell taped onto her collar. and her dog recovered. I have tried this technique on other animals since then, with great success."*
-Shari Lynn, California

photo by Star Dewar

→*"They call me Mr. Sat and I am a handsome nineteen-year-old terra-cotta __Tabby cat__. I admit that I owe my excellent health and good looks to something my mom started experimenting with three years ago, Tachyon Energy. First our water was energized, then we got a Tachyonized Life Pad to sleep on and Tachyon collars. It seemed to be working but the proof came when mom brought home a very skinny stray cat. She had a __raggedy coat__ and __runny eyes__. I thought to myself, "good grief, could that grundgy look be contagious?" Next thing I knew, mom put Tachyonized Water right into her mouth. After only two weeks, the little orphaned Annie's fur started to shine like the rest of us. The bald spots filled in with downy fur. Her leaky eyes cleared up and she was no longer an embarrassment. It was that simple, just a few drops on top of our food morning and night.*

*In the fall, we all rejoiced, because not one of us, including the __dogs__, suffered one bit from the usual dry, itching, hot spots that had plagued us for years at the end of summer. The only thing different in our diets was the Tachyonized Water! It was about that time that our neighbor's cat Moe, got the Tachyon treatment. One night he was __sprayed in the face by an offended skunk__ and could hardly breathe. His owner thought of taking him to the clinic, but decided to call our house wanting to try the Tachyon Water drops first. His nose, throat and lung inflammation cooled quickly. The Tachyonized*

*Life Capsule that she hung from his collar, accelerated his complete recovery, and he still wears it every day.*

*Even my sweetheart, Essence of Pearl, was helped. She was tired and thin and had begun experiencing seizures. We were told that she had almost no red blood cells and the vet thought the end was near. She was given Tachyonized Silica Gel daily and after a few days showed her same old interest in food. Within four weeks she was taken back to the vet's office and shocked them all...her blood was back to normal! The miracle of Tachyon has certainly enhanced the quality of life around here."*
-Star Dewar, for Mr. Sat of California

HOMEOPATHIC.

Homeopathic treatments, available for over two-hundred years, are becoming more mainstream and people now are considering their usage for pets. Basically, homeopathy treats an illness by the stimulation of the body's own healing process, much like a vaccination only without much risk for a reaction. These remedies are prepared from natural plant substances. They are delivered in micro-doses, thereby highly reducing the risk of side-effects or toxicity.

→*"I took in a stray female __cat__ whose fur was in terrible shape. She was really __allergic to fleas__. I have looked for over two years for flea products that were not commercial poisons, to help my cat friends. At first, Betty's coat was in such bad shape that she had to have cortisone shots. Then I started putting fifteen drops of Scratch Free homeopathic in her daily drinking water. Two weeks later I noticed a remarkable improvement in her coat. Hair that broke off two inches above the tail, started growing back and her really thin coat along her backbone also started to thicken. She now has a lush winter coat and is so much more comfortable. She has fewer fleas since I have also used Flea Relief homeopathic remedy."*
-Merilea, California

Since homeopathy views the individual as a whole, symptoms and signs from the body, mind and spirit are all taken into consideration when selecting treatment. For example, if you peel and onion, your eyes burn, your nose runs or you begin to sneeze. If those same symptoms appear when you get a cold, a minute dose of homeopathic Allium cepa (the red onion) would help your body heal itself. There are more than one-hundred double-blind clinical studies which document the efficacy of homeopathic remedies. Dosages are available in tablets, liquids, suppositories and ointments. The most popular form is pellets, taken sublingually (under the tongue). These dissolve quickly are easy to administer to pets.

When you see a homeopathic remedy the dilution will be indicated on the label. X potencies are diluted by using one part of the mother tincture and nine parts alcohol or water. As we continue the series of dilutions we obtain 2X 3X, etc. C potencies are diluted by using one part of the mother tincture and ninety-nine parts of alcohol or water, therefore 2C, 3C, etc. Each succeeding dilution further reduces the potency, although it still may be effective. Different individual indications require different potencies.

Homeopathic medicines need some special consideration. Storage of containers is important. They should be kept away from light and sources of electrical appliances as these can diminish the potency. Do not feed your animal for fifteen minutes either before or after giving the remedy and don't give your dog chocolate (not good for them anyway), as this negates the effect. Make sure your pet is off drugs as antibiotics, antihistamines, anti-inflammatories and anesthetic agents can possibly interfere with homeopathic action. These remedies should not be used unless they have been prescribed by a practitioner familiar with the animal. If you get a reaction to a remedy, you may antidote it with coffee or another homeopathic remedy recommended by your homeopath. Some of the more common homeopathic remedies are listed below.

•**Allium cepa** (Red onion) for colds, flue, violent sneezing, sore throat.
•**Arnica montana** (Mountain daisy) for bruises, traumas, injuries, muscular tiredness and pain.
•**Belladonna** (Deadly nightshade) for fever, colds, flu.
•**Calcarea fluorica** (Calcium fluoride) for joint pain, cysts, lumbago.
•**Calcarea sulphurica** (Calcium sulphate) for burns, boils, eczema.
•**Ferrum phosphoricum** (Iron phosphate) for colds, low fever and congestion, cough.
•**Kali muriaticum** (Potassium chloride) for ear, nose and throat

catarrhal inflammations, runny nose, sore throat, mouth ulcers, dandruff.

•**Kali phosphoricum** (Potassium phosphate) for convalescence following flu or infectious disease, exhaustion from nervousness.

•**Kali sulphuricum** (Potassium sulphate) for colds, yellow nasal discharge, scaly skin eruptions.

•**Natrum muriaticum** (Sodium chloride) for eczema, tendency to catch cold, fright, dandruff.

•**Natrum phosphoricum** (Sodium phosphate) for flatulence, indigestion, belching, vomiting, rheumatism of the knee joint, itching skin.

•**Nux vomica** (Poison nut) for upset stomach, constipation.

•**Pulsatilla** (Wind flower) for nasal congestion, chronic irritation of mucous membranes.

•**Rhus toxicodendron** (Poison Ivy) for rheumatic pain, muscle pain, sprains, flu-like symptoms, poison ivy.

•**Staphysagria** (Stavesacre) for urinary complaints with burning pain on urination, hypersensitivity of genitals, eczema of the scalp or face.

•**Sulphur** (Brimstone) for itchy or burning skin eruptions, rashes, eczema, diarrhea, recurring sties.

→*"My five year old Golden Retriever developed a terrible **skin condition** due to allergies. She lost all her hair on her hind end, tail and legs, and scratched her face raw until it was bloody. I felt so sorry for her, yet I didn't want to resort to antibiotics and steroids. I sought counsel with a homeopathic vet who treated her with acupuncture and nutritional therapy. The first two weeks I didn't see and improvement. Then I purchased a bottle of Newton Labs Homeopathic Skin Drops and gave it to my dog. Her itching began to subside, her skin became healthy and her hair full-bodied again within a few months. She looked younger and more vibrant!"*
-Marie Dizon, California

## CHAPTER 2. CATS AND DOGS

Fifty four million dogs and sixty three million cats in the United States eat primarily what their owners give them. Many do not have a choice. If left to their own devices, most cats and dogs would eat differently out in the wild. Do they know something we don't? Do they really care that pet foods look appealing? Of course, they are attracted by smell, but certain ingredients may not be good for them. They eat it anyway because they have no alternatives. Providing them with fresh meat from the grocery store may not be the best choice either. Hormones and drugs are administered to feedlot animals on a regular basis. FDA regulations state that ten days before slaughter (or before *human* consumption), antibiotic therapy must cease. Are our inspectors enforcing these regulations? Do these "pollutants" end up in the flesh of these feed lot animals and in their meat which you give to your animals? If you prefer to put together your pet's dinner, choose free-range or organically fed meat sources.

Pet food manufactures are allowed to use this same meat plus "road pizza", diseased and pus laden animals, euthanized pets, all labeled "by-products." Also included in pet food are turkey and chicken gullets. They are full of indigestible and potentially harmful materials such as gravel and stones, which can cause diarrhea and blockages in dogs and cats. Metal bands on poultry are not normally removed before processing, and therefore can find their way into your pet's dinner. Also sometimes found in canned pet food, are the identification tags from euthanized pets....a horrible, but realistic eye opener to the lack of control in what goes in your cat or dog's dinner. Natural pet food manufacturers are aware of the hazards of 'tainted' foods and go to great lengths to avoid these meat sources.

→*"Over the twenty-one years of __Veterinary practice__, I have seen the level of health steadily decline in our pet populations, without much information regarding optimum health being provided for those who saw a connection. It seemed everyone was too busy analyzing disease to think of __enhancing health.__ In my practice for years, the natural raw meat diet has maintained vibrancy in the pets of owners who could provide this wholesome diet and saw its real value. I recommend this natural raw meat diet with supplementation; and if that's not possible, PHD Pet Food. The value of PHD is that it succeeds to a large extent in mimicking the natural raw meat diet, as there are no preservatives, it is shipped direct and fresh, and made in smaller, more frequent batches to ensure consumption soon after manufacturing.*

*With this particular brand of food I have seen animals with less skin disease, digestive weakness and upsets. We have seen a higher quality animal; much better coated and alertly settled. Through PHD and the natural raw meat diet, we see not only the pet companion enjoying higher levels of wellness, but the owner enjoying it as well. This makes our job of health care providers to our pets, both fun and rewarding on many levels."*
-Dr. William Pollak, D.V.M., Iowa

## • FOOD

We start off this chapter by letting you know what ingredients many manufacturers add to pet foods. You must be avid label readers if you are going to avoid veterinary bills. Pet foods may contain not only preservatives and additives, but the actual food may contain pus, fecal matter, road kill, virus', cancerous tumors, infected blood, rancid fillers and bacteria. These by-products according to Dr. P.F. McGargle, a veterinarian who has also served as a federal meat inspector, "can include moldy, rancid or spoiled processed meats as well as tissue too severely riddled with cancer to be eaten by people." Dr. Alfred Plechner, D.V.M. comments on by-products stating that "diseased tissue, pus, hair, assorted slaughterhouse rejects, and carcasses in varying stages of decomposition, are sterilized with chemicals, heat and pressure procedures."

In some cases, additional processing with chemical sprays also occurs. Pet food may also contain many of the preservatives, fillers and additives that go into our food, but that does not make them healthy for your pet. The most common additives or harmful ingredients are listed below:

**ALUMINUM.** In 1893, the Public Health Department in Bern, Switzerland warned that "damage to health from the consumption of food or drink from aluminum is to be expected". The Hahnmann Chronic Disease list included 1,160 verified symptoms of aluminum poisoning including infertility, disorders of the blood, skin, nervous, glandular and digestive systems. Cats under the influence of aluminum suffered from a lack of coordination. Aluminum can contribute to diseases similar Alzheimer's, (thought to be an affliction of aluminum toxicity). Aluminum, in the body, will result in an "electrolyte imbalance" and disrupt vital body functions, leading to disease conditions. Animals thought to be aluminum "poisoned" should be treated with large amounts of trace minerals and vitamin C, good chelating agents which help to cleanse the body of this toxin.

Do you serve your pet water in an aluminum bowl? Does their pet food contain aluminum baking powder? Do you wrap scraps of food in aluminum foil? Does your water supplier add aluminum sulphate (a dirt removing agent) to your water? Does your pet food contain plants grown organically in mineral rich soil? If not, the plant may be ingesting aluminum in place of needed minerals. This condition may be due to the fact that acid rain causes the good minerals to wash away leaving behind the heavy metals. Although you don't intentionally give your pet aluminum, many of their symptoms may be attributed to this element which they get through the water, air and food.

**ANIMAL/ POULTRY FAT.** Those scraps of meat which are not fit for human consumption go into pet foods. These rancid fats are heavily preserved with chemicals such as BHT/BHA and Ethoxyquin to prevent further spoilage. Fats in this form are difficult to digest and can lead to a host of health problems including diarrhea, gas, bad breath and vomiting. If fed to young animals, it can permanently affect the sensitive lining of the digestive tract leading to a lifetime of assimilation problems and allergic responses.

**ARTIFICIAL COLOR.** Most people are aware of toxic side effects of artificial colors and flavors from coal tar derivatives such as Red #40, a possible carcinogen, and Yellow #6, which causes sensitivity to fatal viruses in animals.

**BHT/BHA.** These petroleum products are used to stabilize fats in foods. In the process of metabolizing BHA and BHT, chemical changes occur in the body. These changes have caused reduced growth rate and they inhibit white blood cell stimulation. In humans, they exhibit reactions such as skin blisters, hemorrhaging of the eye, weakness, discomfort in breathing, the reduction of the body's own antioxidant enzyme, glutathione peroxidase and may cause cancer.

**ETHOXYQUIN.** This was originally designed as a rubber stabilizer and herbicide and before its approval, the FDA characterized it as a poison. It was first introduced as a grain preservative on feed intended for animals raised for slaughter and not expected to live more than two years. It has been reported to cause liver cancer in dogs and can cause increased mortality and malformations in newborn puppies. It can contribute to skin allergies and some immune related diseases.

**MEAT BY-PRODUCTS.** Called "4D" sources, this type of labeling on pet foods can contain, meat, tissues and insides of animals that are dead, dying, disabled or diseased and not fit for human consumption when they reach the slaughterhouse. This translates to hooves, hides, hair, bones, feathers, beaks, and also can include euthanized pets and road kill. Feeding food which includes these wastes, increases the animals chance of getting cancer and other degenerative diseases not to mention promoting cannibalism. (Mad Cow Disease is thought to be the cannibalistic result of including in cow feed, sheep and cow meat, leading to the eventual disintegration of the brain.) Hormones, steroids and antibiotics in slaughtered animals are active even in "dead " tissues. Some by-products may be a good source of nutrition for your pet, such as organ meats, bones, skin, etc. Unfortunately, because government regulations dictate that the nutritional *and* 4D ingredients must all be labeled by-products, you really are unable to determine exactly what kind of "by-products" are in your food.

**PEANUT HULLS.** An inexpensive bulk-producing source of fiber, that can create chronic constipation and damage the tissues of the colon.

**PESTICIDES.** A must to maintaining a healthy diet, is to avoid pesticides. Found just about everywhere, they are altering our genetic makeup, producing animal and bird mutations, and assuring eventual demise of the planet. Most obvious is the assault to health, manifesting itself as cancer. The E.P.A. now considers many previously approved chemicals to be potentially carcinogenic - 60%

of all herbicides, 90% of all fungicides and 30% of all insecticides currently being used on our farm crops. A list of fruits and vegetables that are most susceptible to contamination from pesticides (unless you choose organic varieties) is listed in order of highest risk of contamination: strawberries, bell, green and red peppers, spinach, cherries, peaches, cantaloupe (from Mexico), celery, apples, apricots, green beans, grapes, cucumbers.

**PROPYLENE GLYCOL.** Used as a de-icing fluid for airplanes, this chemical is added to food and skin products to maintain texture and moisture as well as inhibiting bacteria growth in the product. It also inhibits the growth of friendly bacteria in the digestive system by decreasing the amount of moisture in the intestinal tract leading to constipation and cancer. It can affect the liver and kidneys.

**SALT.** Added as a preservative, salt can irritate the stomach lining, cause increased thirst and aggravate heart and kidney problems through fluid retention. It can also increase blood pressure.

**SODIUM NITRITE.** Used in the curing of meats, this substance participates in a chemical reaction in the body that becomes carcinogenic. It is used also in pet foods to add color.

**SOYBEAN.** Pet food manufacturers add soybean to increase protein content and bulk. It is very difficult to digest and assimilate especially for dogs who lack the proper amino acid needed. The number one allergy in dogs is soy (the number two is wheat, three is corn). High soy diets in animals are evident after surgery, because the stitches don't hold well and infections set in. It is the number one allergic food for dogs and can lead to bloat which is a major killer. Dogs must know this, for in the wild, they do not touch soybeans.

**SUGAR AND OTHER SWEETENERS.** The most common sweeteners in pet foods are beet sugar, corn syrup, molasses and sucrose. They are used as preservatives and have the side effect of creating sugar addicts in pets. They require almost no digestion and are rapidly absorbed into the blood stream. These will provide sugar highs, (just as humans experience) and subsequent lows, inhibit the proper growth of friendly intestinal bacteria, and they virtually shut down the digestive system while being processed. Sugar can also contribute to diabetes and hypoglycemia, cataract development, obesity, dental decay and arthritis. Sugar as well as corn gluten meal, wheat gluten meal, rice gluten meal may be added to pet food to slow down the transition of rancid animal fats. These glues and sweeteners hold the toxins in the food during digestion. The kidneys and the liver work overtime. Noticeable allergic behavior to these substances are indicated when dogs chew their lower backs and lick their feet which have become swollen.

## PROTEIN, CARBOHYDRATES AND FATS.

Nutritional deficiencies can show up in your pet in many ways. The easiest to notice is dry, flaky skin and sparse, coarse, brittle hair coat. Becoming aware of what goes into your pet's food is the first step. Pet food companies have done a lot of research to make sure your animal receives the proper nutrients. We should thank them and learn from them. Pet food manufacturers provide protein by including meat and certain vegetables, especially greens. If you decide to cook for your pet, you may leave out certain ingredients they need. Cats and dogs need different nutrients in different amounts than humans, therefore human diets may not be suitable for Fido or Fluffy. Both dogs and cats need protein in their diets to provide specific animo acids which their bodies are unable to produce in sufficient quantity. Cats, for instance, are unable to manufacture taurine, therefore this must be provided by a meat based diet. A taurine deficient cat can develop feline central retinal degeneration, eventually leading to blindness, low weight, reduced growth and also cause a fatal condition which weakens their heart muscle and cause death. Cats require eleven specific amino acids.

Dogs need ten amino acids in proper balance as well as a high supply of methoinine and tryptophane. Although dogs tolerate vegetarianism better than cats, you still may be creating deficiencies that can lead to illness. Vegetarian diets must contain an excellent source of protein, such as wheat or barley grass, sea vegetables or nutritional yeast.

Animals need carbohydrates which provide the body with energy. If a diet consists of an excessive amount of carbohydrates, the animal can develop diarrhea. Grains commonly used in pet food are wheat and soy. These are highly allergenic and may make a dog

40

chew at the root of his tail and lick his feet. Amaranth and barley would be a better choice. Beet pulp is an excellent source of fiber which paces the rate of digestion and permits water to be properly removed from the colon. It also removes scale from collecting in the colon, is a source of vitamin B and contains micro nutrients.

White rice or Brewers rice are commonly used fillers. They are devoid of nutrients and should be avoided. All grains lose vitamins in storage, and many vitamins in meat may be destroyed in the canning process. To compensate, some manufacturers over-fortify their food with copious quantities of vitamins that most likely are not even assimilated by the body because the enzymes needed for this process, are destroyed when the food is cooked. Allergenic foods may ferment in the colon, sometimes for months creating a very toxic environment. Not only does this create allergies, but it jeopardizes the health of the animal. Detoxifying is the only way to remove this debris, and switching to a premium "no-filler" food may be necessary to accomplish this task and maintain a healthy pet.

→*"In April, a **Rottweiler** breeder called me with her experience with the Hund-N-Flocken Dog Food. She said her dogs were switched from a "junk" food brand and after a short while, some of the dogs **lost weight**, got **bad breath** and the urine and stools smelled awful. Some even expelled **gas** so foul, that the dogs had to be put outside. She had been using the food and was almost ready to give up. Then one day when she was picking up the poop, she noticed pieces of yellow and black. Upon closer examination, she saw kernels of corn and fermenting black pieces of corn. She knew that Hund-N-Flocken didn't contain corn. Then she remembered that eight months ago in September, she had given the dogs some corn cobs to chew on. For eight moths these kernels had been embedded inside the wall of the intestines, fermenting. This went on for a few days, then the stools firmed up and the smell went away."*
-as told to Solid Gold

Their diet also must consist of fats and oils which facilitate the transport and storage of fat soluble vitamins. Some pet food companies use sunflower, safflower and corn oils, high in Omega-6 essential fatty acids (EFA). Both dogs and cats need EFA's, for healthy metabolism, although the unbalancing of essential fatty acids,

(Omega-3 and Omega-6) can lead to disease. If oils high in Omega-6 are not balanced by Omega-3, found in flax, for example, they can cause tumor formations. Flax can stimulate the immune system and act as an antioxidant, as well as balancing the effects of too large a quantity of Omega-6 oils. Fats, which provide EFA's are carriers for fat soluble vitamins, but may become rancid in stored meat or processed food. Rancid fat contributes to cancer and degenerative diseases such as heart problems and arthritis, according to the Surgeon General.  Preservatives such as BHT and BHA are normally added to fight this problem, but a more natural choice would be vitamin C and E.

Manufacturers of the natural pet food products are diligent in preparing properly balanced meals and eliminating the hazardous additives and by-products. It is prudent to trust their formulas. Their research has given them the tools to provide the nutrients each specific breed of animal needs. Supplementing pet diets with certain nutrients is advisable, but let the experts provide the basics.

→*"Quasar looks like a miniature zebra, a black and white brindled coat of short coarse hair from head to tail to toes, a small head, long skinny legs and tiny feed with an oversized broad neck and chest. He's probably part **Whippet and part Terrier.** Conscious of the need for good nutrition, I have always fed Quasar a high quality "premium" dog food, He was on Iams when he was a baby and his coat was always real dry, stiff and course. He shedded a lot and he was always itchy.*

*At the age of four, he began having digestive problems., He started **throwing up** as soon as he would eat his wet food.  He didn't throw up his kibble because he really chewed that. Fearing a blockage in the esophagus, I consulted the vet. He prescribed canned food and medicine, to no avail. Bloodwork revealed an elevated level of eosinophils and finally, the vet finally did a esophageal duodenum duoscopy which allowed them to look all through his stomach and intestines. The pathology report came back...**food allergy** and began treatment with  rounds of cortisone pills and an allergenic diet of kibble made entirely from fish and potatoes.*

*He hated it! He wasn't eating and was losing weight.  He begged for food twenty-four hours a day, so I started searching for a* new food. I asked managers of pet food stores all over town, for a food without preservatives, by-products, corn, wheat or diary. Quasar wouldn't eat them, so I went to the internet looking for another food and was introduced to PHD.

This food he liked and overnight his disposition improved. He's picked up a few pounds and is a happy dog. His blood levels that we've been testing for, came down in the normal range and he hasn't had an intestinal problem since. We never knew what caused his "illness", but I'm not ever putting him back on any of the other foods. It's done so much for his coat and his disposition and his general behavior, that I don't want him to eat anything else. I'm grateful it's all over, and equally grateful that we don't have to play dog food roulette anymore."
-Barbara Bennett, Ohio

→"In general, until ten years ago, I had accepted the conventional western mode of "pet" rearing as the most beneficial. When our eight week old **Samoyed puppy**, Tasha, joined our family, we gave her a diet of only grocery store puppy food. During that time, up until age five, Tasha had numerous attacks of **cystitis and anal gland impactions**. She had chronic **bad breath**, developed a fear of thunder and had attacks of **hyperventilation**. She has a **heart murmur** and from the beginning, was diagnosed as having **congenital hip dysplasia**. Her veterinarian in Minnesota said she wouldn't live very long, mainly because of her hip problems. Our determination to improve her quality of life kept us always looking for options.

We moved to the mountains of Wyoming and here Tasha could take twenty mile hikes and run with the help of two complete hip replacements, but all of her other health problems worsened. Oozing sores began appearing on the outside and inside of Tasha's ears, and bald patches showed up on parts of her body. The sores could be eliminated with topical ointments, but they just kept reappearing. At that point I became desperate, but didn't know what to do for her. One day I picked up a copy of Dr. Pitcairn's 'Guide to Natural Health Care for Dogs & Cats'. He described Tasha's symptoms perfectly and I discovered that we had not been giving Tasha the best possible diet regimen as I had always thought! I followed Dr. Pitcairn's recommendation of detoxification,

43

*followed by a balanced fresh food diet, vitamins, minerals and herbs.*

*She loved her new diet and within a few weeks, her body began to respond positively. Our family was amazed! The oozing sores went away for good. Her hair grew back, and she had no more anal gland impactions, cystitis or bad breath. She kept her phobias, but we were able to strengthen her heart and reduce her arthritis with herbs."*
-Estelle Hummel, Wyoming

## YUMMY TREATS AND VITAMIN PILLS.

Table scraps have gotten a bad rap as being a no-no for animal diets, yet most people are trained by their animals to share their dinners. If your animal is getting proper nutrition through natural canned or dry food, plus supplements, a few table scraps (organic, of course) won't hurt, (depending on what you give them.) Never feed cats or dogs pork, as it is high in preservatives and carries a risk of trichinosis. Raw poultry should be avoided to guard against bacteria infection. Turkey is OK although its high amounts of tryptophan makes lazy animals more lethargic. Tuna fish and cow's milk can trigger allergic reactions in cats and dogs causing skin problems, hyperactivity, and asthma. The oil in tuna can rob your cat of vitamin E resulting in a muscular disease called steatitis. If you give your cat tuna, supplement it with vitamin E.

Chocolate is a no-no for dogs and cats, as it contains theobromine which can be fatal. Also dogs cannot digest the whites of raw eggs, but cooked eggs are OK. Most veggies are a healthy snack. Beans can cause gas unless supplemented with enzymes and anyone who has been around a dog with gas, will avoid beans. Most whole unrefined grains are good for pets if they want to eat them. Vary them, because any grain (especially wheat or corn) eaten on a regular or daily basis, can create allergic reactions. This includes bread, cookies, chips, pasta, doggie cookies, etc. Refined grains and flours (white) should be avoided as they have little nutritional value and actually tax the body as it tries to digest them. Avoid treats with sugar as this substance plays as much havoc on your pet's system as it does on your own.

44

→*"Brunzi is my beautiful __Golden Retriever__.  In October of 1992, I was devastated when I received a biopsy report on a lump that had been removed from Brunzi's face: __squamous cell carcinoma__; Prognosis: guarded.  The thought that I may lose my little five year old "boy" was unbearable to me.  I immediately took him to the vet and he recommended a course of therapy that involved surgically removing all seven lumps that were on his body, implanting small metal disks at each incision and administering pin-point radiation at all cancerous sites. (The reason for the metal disks was to precisely identify each site to radiate). This treatment would occur three times a week for seven weeks and he would have to be anesthetized during each treatment.*

*Needless to say, I was even more devastated after I left the hospital.  I couldn't bear to subject him to the pain and horror for a treatment that did not guarantee his survival. I took him to a holistic veterinarian who addressed the cause of the lumps. What was causing Brunzi's immune system to function poorly?  He put Brunzi on a variety of glandular, enzymatic, vitamin and mineral supplements based on his metabolic nutritional analysis. Brunzi underwent a two week course of immuno-augmentative therapy, and I changed his diet.  Whenever possible I cooked fresh foods for him, using organically grown grains and free-range chickens.  I used a super premium dry dog food and continued his supplement program. For "snacks," I cooked my own organic dog cookies which I started selling as Doggie Divines..*

*This regime worked!  It has now been over three years since Brunzi's cancer diagnosis, and he's never been in better health.  He now has a very important job.  He is a therapy dog who visits his old folk friends at a local nursing home several times a month."*
-Carol Marangoni,  New York


Supplementation is absolutely necessary for animals not fending for themselves in the wild. Cats require a higher concentration of vitamins and essential nutrients than any other animal in the world, including man! Mineral deficiencies, enzyme deficiencies, and essential fatty acid imbalance contribute to a compromised immune system in all species. An excellent indicator of nutritional deficiencies is the skin and coat of an animal. This includes disorders such as excessive shedding, hairballs in cats, bald patches, skin allergies, doggy odor, drippy eyes and hot spots.

In order for nutrients from food or vitamin supplementation to do their job in the body, they must be assimilated. Giving an animal vitamins that they can not break down (due to a lack of enzymes), just means that you will have a nutrient rich litter box. Overcoming deficiencies in the basics of body chemistry will prevent this. This next section contains information regarding the basic nutrients needed for the body to operate as designed.

→*"I am a hardened "pet supplement" skeptic. I own a twelve-year-old **Scottish Terrier** that has been on prednisone injections and oral medication for eight years. I have seen innumerable veterinarians, tried special shampoos, powder supplements - more products and treatments than I could list. My dog Cinder has undergone complete allergy testing, which reached the conclusion that this dog was **allergic to nearly every natural and man-made product on the earth**! Several vets concluded she must be immuno-deficient.*

*She had very little body hair, scratched incessantly, smelled awful and had frequent **ear infections** and staphylococus **skin infections**. My mother gave me some Missing Link whole food concentrates and tried it. I doubled the dosage for the first ninety days and continued giving it to Cinder for a year. I wish you could see my dog now. She has new hair growth, her scratching is greatly reduced and she has had only one ear infection in the past year. My vet is amazed! I changed nothing else in her diet, so now I am a believer in this supplement."*
-Kaye Farrar, Missouri

→*"I love **cats** and there was a litter of kittens born on my farm to a family of "barn" cats. As soon as they were weaned, I took one home and fed her regular cat food along with a supplement, NUPRO. although Pepper wasn't a "barn" cat anymore, she still traveled with me everyday to watch me work at the stables. She became noticeably bigger than her litter-mates and never got any colds or runny eyes like the others. The only vet she ever saw was the barn vet who gave her a rabies shot.*

46

*When she was about two years old, I decided to adopt another "barn" kitten. Before I took him home, I thought it wise to have him tested for __feline leukemia__ because some of the "barn" cats all of a sudden started dying from this disease. Ironically, the new kitten was negative and my Pepper, was positive! I had her tested three more times with identical results. She showed no ill effects and still played like a kitten, but alas, she was positive and my vet told me that she was probably born that way. Pepper Puss is now eight years old, still has a beautiful thick, soft, slate gray coat and continues to amaze myself and the vets that she is still alive and active. I can only attest to the fact that because I'm giving her the live enzymes and amino acids that are found in the NUPRO, she is alive and thriving."*

-Janis Gianforte, New Jersey

## • MINERALS

Most of the cats and dogs on the planet are mineral deficient for reasons specified in *MINERALS in CHAPTER 1*. Minerals and trace elements must be present for growth, development and for all the body processes to work. If your pet is lucky enough to have a conscientious human caregiver, they will trust your judgment in supplying them with complete nutrition. This must include minerals, in the form of supplements added to their drinking water or food.

Animals' immune systems have responded to mineral treatment and many sick pets received a speedy recovery, but stress, illness and environmental assaults can upset the mineral balance in our animals creating many ailments. We, as owners, can also cause sickness in our pets, by playing doctor and administering single minerals without regard to their effect on other minerals or on the body. As stated in *MINERAL IMBALANCES in CHAPTER 1* precautions should be taken to have your animal tested for mineral imbalances and then apply a proper mineral supplementation program. As a maintenance procedure, add minerals to their diet through a properly balanced trace mineral supplement. This will assure that their bodily functions operate properly, that their antioxidant enzymes are strong to fight infections and that their immune systems stay strong. The following story depicts one success of treatment with minerals

→ *"At the tender age of eight years, our __dog__, Heidi began displaying the classical symptoms of Hip Dysplasia. Our next door neighbor, a woman who was originally a registered nurse, and now a D.V.M., informed me that Heidi had the onset of severe __Hip Dysplasia__. She felt the best I could do was to put Heidi to sleep, as there is no known cure for this problem. Shortly thereafter, I saw a couple who were patients of mine and who ran a dog kennel for many years. I told them of my quandary regarding our beloved Heidi.*

*They mentioned that there was experimental research being done at a major veterinary school in Scotland and that they would make inquiry. Several weeks later I received a very big package of research material on Hip Dysplasia. It disclosed two major areas of concern. The quantity of calcium in the body and the absorption factors regarding this calcium. I recalled from my naturopathic training, that all animals and humans have the same basic nutritional needs. I immediately started supplementing her diet with a good calcium-magnesium citrate and most important of all, a true electrolyte solution, Pet-Lyte.*

*After several weeks, I began to notice subtle, improvements in my dog, such as standing easier and walking straighter. Suffice to say, that within several months, my eight year old Heidi became a puppy again, no longer looking like the tired old aching dog she was! Many years later, at the ripe old age of sixteen, our beloved Heidi was laid to rest. We are now retired and maintain a small organic farm in Florida with our Heidi "Two". She is eight years old and has no signs of that horrible disease. We supplement her diet with electrolytes as a major aid in calcium absorption and several additional nutrients. "*
Dr. I. (Gerald) Olarsch, N.D., Florida

→ *"I recently received a story from a woman who has a __Boxer__, male. He caught __Parvo__ from the vaccination, when he was six weeks old. When the diarrhea started, she immediately tried a supplement, Nupro Custom Electrolyte Formula. He never developed a fever and never vomited, but ultimately had to have major intestinal surgery and three blood transfusions, his spleen and a few other things done, all by the age of nine weeks. Because of the supplement, he never got dehydrated!*

*After the surgery, the vet called and told her to come and pick him up and take him home, because no other dog in the country has survived this type of surgery and it would be better if he died at home. She again started the Nupro Electrolyte Formula right away and the vets were shocked at his total and complete recovery. He is now three years old and has one major and two single points towards his championship. Everyday is a miracle for him and without the electrolytes, she doesn't think he would have survived!"*
-Janis Gianforte, New Jersey


• **ENZYMES**

As we mentioned in *ENZYMES in CHAPTER 1*, enzymes are a key factor in preventing debilitating illness in your cat or dog. Since the natural enzymes in food are killed when food is cooked or processed (dry kibble), your pet's body must supply digestive enzymes. Eventually, the pancreas gets tired of doing this extra work and either gives up or develops disease. Supplementation is a key to better digestion for pet, and enzymes are so easy to give. Enzymes also break down vitamin supplements so that they can be absorbed. For instance, pet food manufacturers sometimes add zinc in a form that is unavailable for absorption. Adding enzymes make those nutrients easier to absorb. Stories of enzyme supplementation being a key factor in restoring health are told all the time.

→*"Sarah Bone is an **Old English Sheep Dog** who is now nine years old...going on three! Sara is very happy and healthy, but unfortunately was not always this way. About eighteen or twenty months ago, Sara developed a **very serious skin disorder**. She had red pustules on her stomach and scaly, scabby sores on her back which bothered her so much she was tearing her hair and skin off for relief.*

*We took Sara to our local (well-respected) veterinarian, who immediately injected her with steroids and prescribed antibiotics and oral steroids which would "make her comfortable and heal the wounds." After about a year on both medications, her condition remained basically unchanged. As soon as the medication was decreased, the skin erupted again. Meanwhile, Sara's blood count was horrible and the vet was concerned that he may have to operate because of her spleen. He felt that her immune system was unable to fight off whatever was causing the skin problem so he started her on weekly injections of something that I believe he called SPL.*

*As you can imagine, Sara felt horrible. By the time she was eight-and-a-half years old, she appeared truly geriatric and was hardly able to walk around the block. I called the University of North Carolina Veterinary School to see if there was a "doggie dermatologist" there that would take a look at her. They said they would start by placing her on a hypoallergenic diet for about ten weeks and then test her for allergies, but they needed a recommendation from my vet to proceed. My veterinarian was outraged that I would take my pet somewhere else and would not give me the referral. I decided to take matters into my own hands.*

*I discontinued the antibiotics and shots, and weaned her off the steroids. I developed my own dog food recipe which includes fresh and frozen veggies, legumes, organic brown basmati rice, non-fat cheese, virgin olive oil, garlic and other spices and grains. I added a powdered barley grass supplement, Barley Dog, containing thousands of enzymes. Sara Bone now jogs half a mile every morning and can hardly sit still. Her skin is clear, her coat is shiny and healthy. Her eyes have the whitest whites and her toes (which were almost devoid of hair, had the hair grow back and she stopped chewing on them. Sara no longer scratches all the time. We thought that the diet change might be solely responsible until I ran out of Barley Dog and Sara went a week without! After the scratching and reappearance of a red pustule on her chest, I am pleased to know that she is back on the barley enzyme supplement."*
-Lori E., North Carolina


→*"We have been using Prozyme for approximately one year now and the difference in our eight year old **Siberian Husky** is remarkable, to say the least. About a year ago, we were dealing with a completely different animal. **He could barely walk** and it was impossible for him to climb up our stairway at night to our bedroom. We had a complicated dilemma in that he would not sleep*

50

anywhere other than by my side. If I fell asleep in my daughter's room at night, he would invariable find me in there, and I would awaken in the morning to find him sleeping next to me on the floor.

When I moved from my daughter's room at night back into our own bedroom, he would follow. When the **hip dysplasia** became worse, he reached a point where he could not climb the stairs at all. He would lay at the bottom of the stairs and whine insufferably for hours. We couldn't carry him up the stairs because of his weight, and because we were fearful of it causing even greater harm to him. I tried sleeping downstairs at night to bring him some comfort, but that was NOT a long-term solution.

He was only seven years old when this problem became so bad I decided to reach out for help. Our veterinarian suggested costly shots and possibly surgery which we didn't believe was a viable solution to the problem. Our vet also recommended giving him multiple doses of aspirin throughout the day and increasing it at night. The aspirin showed no sign of relieving any of his discomfort. He got tired of sleeping downstairs by himself and devised a way of creeping up the stairs at night, by turning around and moving up the stairway backwards. He would sit down on his bottom and then use his front legs to balance himself while he would slowly raise his back legs up to the next step, then sit down again and do it all over again. This took an insufferable amount of time and was terrible to watch each evening. We'd all give a sigh of relief each night as he made it up one more time and wondered how long we would be able to watch him continue to suffer in this way.

One afternoon, I found myself turning to TV-38, a religious station in our area, to see a video of another Siberian Husky with hip dysplasia. I watched before my eyes, the video of his improvement from the previous video. The product that they had been using was Prozyme, so we decided to try it to see if it could possibly make a difference. I am writing to tell you that our Husky now trots up the stairs at night and even several times during the day. In the past, he would never go upstairs except at night, even if we were up there for long periods of time, because of the difficulty. Now if we go up, he goes up. And I recently spent a weekend afternoon with him in our backyard watching him run and play as if he were a pup again. I stood in amazement as I watched him repeatedly run around the yard and up on top of the deck. What a

*blessing this product has been in our lives. Believe me when we say, enzymes were an answer to our prayers. "*
-Michael & Elizabeth Grinn, Illinois

## • VITAMINS AND OTHER NUTRIENTS

Pets need minerals, essential fatty acids and enzymes and also other nutrient supplementation. Steven Hartmann of Green Foods Corporation says during an interview by Dr. Anthony J. Cichoke (Health Food Business, July 1995)," Despite manufacturer claims to the contrary, modern processing methods used in the pet food industry can destroy the vital vitamins necessary to maintain optimum health and live enzymes that animals require for proper digestion." Vitamins and minerals provided by ingredients in commercial pet food are often variable. Grains lose vitamins in storage and niacin (B3) and Thiamine (B1) found in meat, are destroyed during the canning process. Dry foods are made with an extruder, grinding the mixture together, adding water and steam, cooked at high temperatures and then having fat or animal tissue coatings that have been chemically or enzymatically predigested, applied to enhance the palatability. Vitamins must now be added back and although the manufacturers try hard, the level of the various vitamins, especially the antioxidants, might not be sufficient to maintain optimal health.

Animals, like humans, need to supplement their diets today. Probiotics, vitamins, nutritional yeast and garlic, greens, other nutrient supplements all have their place in the balancing the body for maintaining health and curing ills. In most cases, supplementation is definitely beneficial to your pet. Dogs and cats vary in nutritional requirements so vitamin and mineral supplements are formulated with those differences in mind. For instance, cats require a higher concentration of vitamins and essential nutrients that any other animal. They need a good supply of calcium and phosphorus in balanced amounts. Cats (unlike dogs) do not have the ability to convert beta carotene to vitamin A therefore they require preformed vitamin A.

Vitamin C is normally manufactured by the animals if given the proper balance of nutrients, but during times of stress or illness, supplementation may be necessary. Dogs with joint disorders, stiffness and arthritic conditions have been shown to improve significantly, during clinic trials where calcium ascorbate was administered. This vitamin is also useful in cats to protect them against a common ailment, cystitis (urinary gravel).

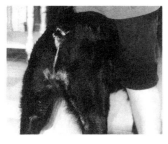

→*I became the adopter of a three year old __Flat Coated Retriever bitch__ on July 24, 1995. When she came to me, she had __no hair at all on the back of her legs, and her hind quarters.__ Her back was red and raw with __scabs__. She also had a few totally bald patches from scratching, something she did almost incessantly. As you can see from the "after" photo, in just eight weeks her coat has improved tremendously. The backs of her legs are now feathered, the redness and scabs have disappeared. I saw improvement almost immediately after beginning feeding her a premium dog food and adding one and one half scoops of Nupro supplement to her diet. In September 1996, she won an AKC Championship!*

*I also use Nutri-Pet Research electrolyte product before shows and during hot weather. It is amazing how "up" the dog stays. I would recommend it highly for anyone who shows their dogs, especially for traveling. It helps to keep the dog from dehydrating and improves energy as well.*
-Terry Ann Fowler, Michigan


→*" We have a large colony of rescued __greyhounds__ that serve as blood donors in our not-for-profit blood bank and then are adopted to pet homes. Some of these greyhounds have low-grade chronic problems with their __skin and haircoat__ (patchy alopecia, thin or brittle hair). For animals showing particular problems, we have been adding Missing Link supplements to their twice daily feeding and have seen a significant improvement. Focal areas of hyperemia on the skin have faded and any irritated "hotspots" have dried up rapidly.*

*We have also noted improved quality, shine and texture to the coat and that areas of alopecia have started to grow hair again.*

*Because the greyhound has relatively thin skin that is easily torn, it is important to have their skin in optimum condition to reduce any tendency for scratching and to promote hair growth as a cover."*
-W. Jean Dodds, D.V.M., California


→*"I have two red __poodles__ and have tried everything from vegetable oil to garlic, and although I'm sure it was healthy for them, the dogs showed no effects on their __coat__. I tried Maximum Protection Formula vitamins and minerals and it showed almost immediate results such as a gleam in their eyes, white, strong teeth, soft and supple skin without any dryness or flaking, and soft, fluffy fur with a shine (it's hard to get a shine in their fur). Also, they never get fleas or ticks anymore."*
Lorrie Cancillieri, New Jersey


## GREENS AND GARLIC.

When animals forage, they include greens in their diet. Domestic cats and dogs may nibble on nothing more than grass, but this gives us an indication of their need for chlorophyll, known as concentrated sun power. Chlorophyll is to the plant as blood is to the animal. It is a natural blood builder and also heals wounds by stimulating repair of damaged tissues and inhibiting growth of bacteria. It has been known to cure acute infections of the respiratory tract and controls halitosis. As an antioxidant, it even has shown to nullify the effects of environmental and food pollutants. It can actually be more effective than vitamin C, E, or A and be an effective preventive measure for cancer. Chlorophyll is found in greens, especially when the plant is young before it begins to grown branches. Sprouts are an excellent source of chlorophyll and are easy to grow year round.

Chlorophyll is also abundant in cereal grasses such as wheat and barley. These are easily obtainable in supplement form and contain high amounts of protein. Grasses are rich in magnesium, considered to be an excellent blood and kidney cleanser and blood cooler in hot weather, rich in antioxidants and due to its high enzyme content, wheat and barley grass are powerful detoxifiers. Many vegetables contain incomplete proteins and can't be totally utilized by the body. Wheat and barley grasses contain all twenty amino acids and therefore are a bioavailable source of protein.

→*" I have a four and one-half year old __English Springer Spaniel__ named Harry. With proper care, Springers are known to have beautiful soft coats. Unfortunately, they are also prone to __dry skin and skin allergies.__ Harry is no exception. I have tried bathing him with oatmeal baths, tea tree oil, and medicated shampoos. I have tried sprays and lotion, and brush him daily. This year, his dry skin developed dandruff and a dull, rough coat. The skin on his stomach was bright pink and full of tiny scabs where he'd been scratching and biting.*

*On the internet, I discovered information on a product, Barley Dog, and ordered it. Within a few day's of giving Harry this supplement, his coat was soft and shiny without a speck of dandruff, no more pink stomach or tiny scabs. When I walk him, people actually stop and comment on his beautiful coat. I'm sure the ingredients in Barley Dog are the reason."*
-Elizabeth Narmore, California

Sea vegetables, algae and Chlorella are also an excellent source of not only chlorophyll, but minerals and vitamin C. Kelp is high in minerals especially calcium, iodine, potassium, and magnesium and is a good source of vitamin C. It is effective against respiratory infections, intestinal and urinary problems. Its iodine content aids digestion and increases assimilation of fatty elements in food. Kelp causes better retention and utilization of calcium and phosphorus contributing to shiny coat and skin health. Chlorella is a single cell algae It is rich is chlorophyll, minerals, vitamin A, B2, B3, B6, high in protein and vitamin C. It has been an effective treatment for ulcers, cancer, colds and vicious bacteria as well as an excellent immune booster. Blue green algae and spirulina are also excellent sources of proteins, vitamins and minerals. Since your pets can't ask for greens, you may want to consider adding one of the powdered or pill supplements to their diet.

Garlic has been an all around remedy for hundreds of years. It is effective against bacteria, virus, fungus' and parasites. It has also been tested as a treatment for cancer where it was found that aged garlic extract was more effective than raw garlic. Aged garlic extract has the allicin (the smelly part) removed. Allicin was once thought to be the most effective part of garlic. New studies confirm that is not the case, whereby allicin can actually be toxic and kill cells. Aged garlic extract is a more effective form of this superb antioxidant herb. Animals are treated with garlic for fevers, pulmonary, gastric and skin conditions, rheumatism, parisitical infestation, worms, tick, lice. When taken with nutritional yeast, garlic can be an effective flea repellent as the skin takes on an odor that the fleas don't like.

→*"One day a few months ago, I noticed my **dog**, Nikki, beginning to limp. Upon examining the paw, I found one **toe red and swollen,** but nothing to indicate what the problem was. I continued to watch her for another few days as her activity level decreased due to the pain and increased swelling in her toe. We take Nikki to a very progressive and good vet clinic and they have helped her a lot, but on this visit, the results proved inconclusive. Two days later she could not even walk on the foot and refused to move except when absolutely necessary. The toe had swollen to about the size of her entire foot.*

*Returning to the vet clinic, they proceeded to cut open the toe for further examination. A small, seed-size lump was found, but I was informed that this was not the cause of the pain and swelling. No real cause for the problem was found. They heavily medicated the paw and wrapped it up. We were given medication and asked to return in two days. She continued to move only as necessary. We returned to the vet clinic in two days and the bandage was removed. The incision was open wide exposing infected tissue and the swelling had not decreased at all. They were baffled!*

*As a last resort, they would consider removing the toe completely, which is not an uncommon practice in dogs. Our instructions were to put a sock over it to prevent her from licking the incision, continue with antibiotics and keep them informed. We all had been taking Kyolic Aged Garlic Extract capsules, but I had heard of amazing healing powers of the Kyolic Aged Garlic Extract Liquid. I decided to try it on Nikki's toe. No one was going to take my dog's toe without a fight.*

*I soaked a cotton ball with the plain liquid Kyolic and held in on the incision for a minute. I also dribbled some in the wound. Then I placed the sock over her foot. I also gave her some Kyolic in a dish to lap up. I also gave her 6 capsules a day. By the end of the second day the swelling was going down and the incision was closing up. By the end of the third day, the incision was completely*

*closed and the toe was almost its normal size. We returned to the vet clinic five days later and they were absolutely amazed at the condition of the toe. They had been at a loss for helping Nikki and were only too pleased that the Kyolic had worked."*
-Dawn Hoffman, Ohio

HEALING NUTRIENTS.

•**Alfalfa** is considered highly nourishing in addition to being a rich source of trace minerals. It is high in chlorophyll which can have a cleansing action on the body, detoxifying and preventing odors.

•**Aloe Vera** has remarkable healing powers both internally and externally as a cleanser, detoxifier and normalizer. It can penetrate all seven layers of the skin, permeating to the germinal layer carrying nutrients, is rich in mucopolysaccharides (pulls water out of the air to moisten skin), and contains anti-inflammatory agents. It is used for treatment of wounds, scar prevention, eczema, burns, rashes, swellings, abrasions, irritation and itching.

•**Antioxidants** such as vitamins C, E, A, fight infection and disarms free radicals. They may help prevent cataracts. Vitamin C helps promote healing, is an immune strengthener and helps reduce arthritis pain. It works best when taken with vitamin E, one of nature's powerful antioxidants. Vitamin E is added to pet food to retard spoilage. Vitamin E is found in the oil of the wheat germ, corn, sunflower and cottonseed, egg yolks and liver. A report from the Aequus Veterinary Service reported the following success with antioxidants and vitamins:

→*CASE 1:  16 yr. old Persian mix* **cat**.
*Complaint:* **Difficulty walking, anorexia, weight loss, irritable personality**
*Exam: Marked loss of range of motion in both coxofemoral joints, decreased lateral motion of most lumbar vertebrae, poor, dry hair coat, 20% below ideal weight, abdominal palpation revealed kidneys slightly small and firm.*
*Treatment: Cat was adjusted in lumbosacral area, all lumbars and lower cervicals. Owner was recommended to put cat on raw meat diets with vegetables and grains. The only supplement cat was placed on was Vetri-Science Nu-Cat feline vitamins with additional supplementation with 400 IU Vitamin E.*

*Response:* Owner reported that cat was markedly better within a week in both its activity level and appetite. At 3 months an exam reported the cat continues to progress well. Hair coat has improved dramatically and cat's attitude is much improved. She wants to be part of the family again. Acupuncture has been added to the treatment regimen.

→*CASE 4: 13 yr. old domestic short hair cat*
*Complaint:* **Kidney failure, anorexia, emaciation, stiffness**
*Exam:* Cat showed 15-20% loss if ideal body weight. Skin is dry and dull with dander flakes. Approximately 8% dehydration was estimated. During crisis last summer veterinarian recommended euthanasia. Cat was eating only tuna at time of exam.
*Treatment:* Owner was taught how to administer subcutaneous saline fluids to maintain hydration. Cat was acupunctured every other day for two weeks for renal failure. Severe nutritional compromise was also diagnosed due to diet. Cat was found to eat vegetable/meat baby foods (organic origin) and was put on them. Added to the diet were blue-green algae, Vetri-Science LinoPrim (essential fatty acid Evening Primrose Oil) and Vetri-Science Cell Advance 440.
*Response:* Cat has improved considerably considering the severe degenerative state that the cat is in. He now talks to the owners, comes to meals with other cats and is more willing to interact. The cat's coat color has deepened and dander is resolving. Owners are reasonable about expectations and are not trying for a cure, but improvement in this cat shows importance of maintaining proper nutrition. Cat is slowly putting on weight.

•**Bee pollen** is rich in nutrients and live enzymes  Pollen is a potent source of RNA and DNA. It also contains abundant quantities of rutin, which strengthens capillaries, is a blood builder and strengthens fertility in breeding as well as combating allergies. It may control the runaway growth of cancer cells because of its antioxidant vitamins A and E.. High in lecithin, bee pollen helps increase brain functions, a plus for senior animals. It is richer in amino acids than any animal source containing five to seven times more amino acids than beef, eggs and cheese of equal weight. This is significant because the protein quality in most commercial pet foods is very low. Because of its vast range of nutrients, bee pollen is extremely beneficial for the immune system.

→*DeeDee Jonrowe, a top racer in the Iditarod and Alpirod races for sled dogs, feeds bee pollen to her champion team.*

•**Biotin** is a B vitamin that is thought to act as a coenzyme and is necessary for certain reactions incorporating amino acids into protein, as well as being essential for thyroid, adrenal and nervous system health. Biotin deficiencies in dogs and cats can appear as skin disorders, loss of hair, eczema as well as weak hindquarters and stiffness. Sometimes these deficiencies are misdiagnosed as dermatitis or flea bites and drugs are administered as a "cure" which can further aggravate the biotin loss. Biotin loss can be provoked by the animals eating raw egg whites which contain avidin (the protein that interferes with biotin absorption). Cooking the egg will destroy the avidin, therefore if you give your animals eggs, make sure they are cooked.

•**Blue-green algae** provides amino acids, minerals, enzymes, vitamins and chlorophyll. A report from Aequus Veterinary Services, Kimberly Henneman, DVM, shows success with antioxidants, essential fatty acids and blue-green algae:

→*"One of my clients had an eight-month old Great Dane pup with an extremely severe skin condition. The pup had an extremely high fever, sores all over his body and hardly any hair. His body was so sore he did not want to even move. He had even given up scratching as it was too uncomfortable. The vet had suggested that she put him down because he was not responding to any medication. We discussed what we might try on the pup and I told her about a previous success with a show pup that had a similar condition only not as severe. I suggested Cell Tech Super Blue Green™ Algae. She jumped at the hope that the algae might help, as we did not think he would make it through the night.*

*We also added enzymes, acidophilus and co-enzyme Q-10 to his regime. I had them mix the contents of the capsules with water and syringe the concoction into the pup's mouth several times throughout the day. I also had them make up a solution of the acidophilus and algae and sponge that over all the sores and*

*pustules. He made it through the night and the next day he had only a mild fever. Within several days, he was up and dashing about. A week later, his skin was healing beautifully and his appetite is back."*
-Written by Sharon Trump for Vicky Slezak, Florida Ind. Distr.CTA NO. 116556

•**Borage, black current and evening primrose oil** are high sources of gamma linoleic acid (GLA) identical to Omega 3 EFA except for its bonding structure and therefore gives similar health benefits.

•**Boswella** is a potent herb for inflammatory disease such as arthritis. It effectively shrinks inflamed tissue, the underlying cause of pain, by improving the blood supply to the area affected. This gummy extract from the Boswella tree is being used on horses and dogs with great success. It acts by mechanism similar to non-steroidal groups of anti-arthritic drugs with a plus being, very few side effects. Dogs with spinal arthritis and hip displasure respond favorably when maintenance dosages are given.

•**Bovine cartilage** has become one of the few substances known to man to have healing properties to accelerate clinical cell growth for skin wounds, torn ligaments, muscle repair, joint deformity and bone degeneration. More concentrated than regular bovine cartilage (ground cartilage), Proteoglycans (bovine cartilage proteins) are effective at treating cancers, arthritis, rheumatism because of its anti-inflammatory properties. The best proteoglycans are found in cows raised organically. After twenty-five years of testing, no side-effects have been recorded.

→*"Recently, LH Black Face, a well known **greyhound** star who raced the dog-track circuit in Florida, suffered from a **lame ankle** which as a consequence affected the shoulder. His owner wanted to bring him back into racing condition. He administered ARTHROFLEX, bovine cartilage, for thirty days. Astounding results were realized. The dog which was basically finished, was back at the track, not only competing, but winning. Already out of eleven races, LH Black Face has marveled South Florida's racing enthusiast by placing three winners, three seconds and two fourths. This is truly an amazing accomplishment since the dog would have been permanently retired due to its poor physical condition."*
-Ray Caldwell, Florida

•**Cat's Claw** (Una de Gato), a rainforest herb that produces oxindole alkaloids proven to enhance phagocytosis (ability of white blood cells and macrophages to attack toxins). An antioxidant, it works to relieve tumors, arthritis, diabetes, allergies, respiratory and circulatory problems and as an immune booster.

•**Cereal Grass.** Wheat and barley grasses contain all twenty amino acids and therefore are a bioavailable source of protein. Dehydrated cereal grasses contain 25% protein, whereas (for an equivalent weight), milk contains 3%, eggs 12% and steak 16%. Vegetable proteins have been considered incomplete (not containing all twenty amino acids). Cereal grass is different according to Pines, manufacturers of wheat and barley grass supplements, claiming they contain all the essential amino acids in amounts which make its protein usable to the body. It also contains high amounts of iron, vitamin C and bioflavonoids.

→*" Recently, I took care of some* **German Shepherds**. *One of them, Shep, was in terrible shape. Several years ago Shep sustained an* **injury**. *Due to the pain that would come and go, he began to visibly age. Just to get him up and* **walking was a great effort** *on his part and mine. His eyes were dull and lifeless and he carried himself very protectively. Shep had to be coaxed to eat and rarely finished what he was given, despite the fresh raw meat added to his kibble.*

*His owners had recently begun adding a newly developed dog food supplement containing active enzymes in a base of juiced and dried cereal grasses and active acidophilus, with his food. I was asked to continue this program. Shep was returned to his owner after their trip, and when I saw him three weeks later, he was a different dog! He was running after his ball, jumping and leaping, his eyes were bright and his appetite had returned. The only change in Shep's care was the continued use of the active enzyme food supplements. "*
-Lynne Girrell, Michigan

•**Coenzyme Q10** is found in every food source including plants, animals and microbes. However, the form of coenzyme Q that is needed for animals comes only from vertebrate sources (Q10) such as mackerel, salmon and sardines. Animals can make their own Q10 from vegetables that contain coenzyme Q9, yeast's Q6, and fungi

Q7. Long term storage of foods can break down these Q enzymes and make them unavailable to the body, therefore supplementation may be necessary. Coenzyme Q is required for energy production by cells and is an important antioxidant. It is helpful for heart disease, allergies, periodontal disease, cancer and to bolster the immune system. Veterinarians use this nutrient to treat chronic skin diseases.

•**Flax** is a superb source of Omega 3 essential fatty acids. These essential fatty acids contribute to a lustrous coat, eliminates hot spots, bald spots, helps prevent dry skin and heals red and raw areas. Flax oil or flax meal are excellent sources of these life enhancing nutrients. Read *HEALING FATS in CHAPTER 1.*

→*"One of our customers had such great results with using Fortified Flax for her arthritis, that she gave it to her_dog who had a terrible fungus. She found it worked so well that his hair stopped falling out in clumps and the fungus disappeared. A plus was that his coat became more shiny and beautiful than before. Our dog, Tasha was troubled with severe diarrhea so I tried the Fortified Flax, and by the next morning, the problem was gone. Some letters we have received from users that have given it to their pets, said they become more energetic with the flaxseed."*
-Milly Nelson, Wisconsin

•**Glucosamine,** a basal membrane builder know to be an effective treatment for many tissue disorders. It helps restore the thick, gelatinous nature of the fluids and tissues in and around the joints and is used as treatment for damaged and inflamed muscles, slipped disc, osteo-arthritis, and intestinal wall irritations. Usage of this substance comes from the Anne Arundel Veterinary Hospital in Maryland:

→ *A three year old male yellow **Labrador** was seen in May of 1993 for diarrhea. The dog proved negative for hook worms, but **ulcerative colitis** was suspected. The dog was treated, unsuccessfully, with a sulfonamide drug Flagyl®, Lomotil® and a diet of Hills Prescription Diet® Canine W/D®. In August of 1995, the dog was started on a supplement containing N-Acetyl Glucosamine (Vetri-Science Multi-Source Glucosamine®). Six* *months have passed and the dog has only had one episode of diarrhea.*

•**Hops** are taken from a plant that winds itself around willow and other trees. They are known for their antiseptic properties, helping all digestive ailments, general debility and skin eczema. It is also used as a natural worming agent, sedative, appetite stimulant and use of hops may have a definite effect on smooth muscles, particularly that of the digestive tract, being good for chronic bowel disorders.

•**Iodine**, found in sea vegetables aids digestion and increases assimilation of fatty elements in food. It is know to assist in calcium and phosphorus retention promoting a better skin and coat condition.

•**Kelp** is a great source of vitamins, iodine, minerals and trace elements which act as catalysts to aid vital enzyme reactions. It is good for bones, teeth and muscle, brings out the highlights in coat color in for older pets, helps arthritic conditions. It is particularly rich in iodine as well as other essential minerals. It influences the blood, raising the red blood count, and has treated thyroid problems.

•**Lecithin** is a fat burner and promotes alertness as well as steadying the nerves.

•**Natural care products.** In addition to feeding your pet healthy food, you should be aware of applications of chemical products that are used to repel fleas and for grooming. Not all shampoos are good for animals, especially cats who will lick their fur and ingest the shampoo ingredients. Avoid all shampoos with chemicals in them and seek out those having nutritional ingredients such as aloe, jojoba oil or herbs. Make sure your flea collar is an herbal type (not chemically based), and never use chemical flea sprays on your pet.

•**Nutritional (Bakers') yeast.** Primary (not Brewer's) yeast is a high source of B vitamins (thiamin, riboflavin, niacin, pyridoxine, Pantothenic acid, biotin and folic acid), amino acids (lysine and tryptophan which are deficient in grains), and minerals (including molybdenum, chromium and selenium, which are deficient in most diets). Nutritional yeast promotes hair growth, helps in repelling fleas, and supports the immune system, and can prevent your dog from blowing coat, even in the summer. Baker's yeast is preferred over Brewer's yeast because it is grown under carefully controlled conditions on purified mixtures of cane and beet molasses. This allows nutritional uniformity and produces higher levels of B vitamins. Brewer's yeast is a by-product of the brewing industry obtained from sediment left over after fermentation. It is harvested after fermenting as many as ten or eleven batches of beer and may contain a number of unknown yeast types, some not so healthy.

•**Oxygen Enhancers** are useful, especially for animals who exert themselves, such as racing dogs or horses. Adding oxygen supplements to your pet's diet helps enhance nutrient absorption and can be a powerful respiratory aid.

•**Probiotics** such as Lactobicillus acidophilus and other probiotics are found naturally in the gastrointestinal tract of healthy animals. These microorganisms provide "friendly" bacteria in the colon to assist with digestion, elimination and restoration of proper flora balance after upset or illness. They also produce lactic acid and keep the colon environment slightly acid to prevent the growth of harmful organisms. Environmental, nutritional or situational changes can disrupt and decrease these beneficial micro-organisms in the digestive tract. Without the good bacteria, harmful strains can take over causing intestinal problems. Supplementation may be necessary, especially after usage of drugs, such as beneficial-flora killing antibiotics, have been administered for illness.

→*" I have recently had a three pound __Pom__ pick up a __virus__ and couldn't control the __diarrhea__ until I managed to get down two capsules of Kyo-dophilus on a bit of baby food. I had to nurse her round the clock to be sure she took fluids (by eyedropper) and sneak in a little bit of the baby food, I had nursed her for forty-eight hours without success in stabilizing the bowel and stomach. After giving her the Kyo-dophilus, she settled down for a good four hours before a normal bowel movement. I continued its usage for a week and each day she continued to improve. I believe it helped to save my "Schweet's" life. A three pound Pom doesn't have much luck surviving after two or three days of dehydration and diarrhea. She's fat and happy again and trying to rule the roost."*
-Toni Dickerson, Maryland

•**Royal Jelly** is the white milky substance produced by worker bees, that feed the queen and increase her size sixty percent. Royal jelly contains taurine, an essential nutrient for cats. The effects of royal jelly on animals have included dramatic improvements in arthritic conditions, better coats, relief from insomnia, increased energy and a speedy recovery after surgery. It also contains 10-hydroxy-2-decenoic acid, which has been shown to have powerful antimicrobial characteristics that my enhance the anti-inflammatory effect of royal jelly against arthritis.

•**Spriulina.** This planktonic blue-green algae has a sixty-two percent animo acid content, is the world's richest natural source of vitamin B-12 and is different from most algae in that it is easily digested. Scientific studies show that spirulina strengthens the immune system, causes regression and inhibition of cancers as well as inhibiting viral replication,. When the cell membrane is attacked by a virus it normally penetrates it causing illness. Spirulina prevents this penetration, thereby making the virus unable to reproduce. It is then rendered harmless by the body's defense system. It is also high in GLA essential fatty acid, stimulating growth in animals and making skin and coat shiny and soft. It feeds the beneficial intestinal flora and is excellent in alleviating symptoms of arthritis. Spirulina is also good at treating parasitic or bacterial infections.

•**Supplements for Hip and Joint problems** have been tested and results indicate that shark cartilage, calf bone meal, bioflavonoids, rutin, collagen concentrates, antioxidants and minerals are an effective treatment in many degenerative and inflammatory conditions. They provide the building blocks required by the body to repair its own articular cartilage and reverse the deterioration of connective tissue. It is also thought that combinations of these nutrients can strengthen ligaments and keep calcium in elemental form so that bone spurs don't occur as hard deposits in the joint.

→*"Winston is a twelve year old __Springer Spaniel__, who had lost a lot of his "spring". Four years ago he was operated on for OCD bone chips in his elbow. Then three years ago, his X-rays showed moderate __hip dysplasia__. By then, his suffering had increased so intensely that there were periods when he cried every morning when he tried to get up out of bed. Once or twice a week, he would refuse to get up at all.*

*The vets I contacted, gave little hope. They said my options were shots of pain-killing steroids or hip replacement surgery. I wasn't willing to believe that nothing else could be done, so I started working with naturopathic health care professionals. We settled on a combination of imported New Zealand Shark tissue concentrates, vitamin C, Pantothenic acid, and bromelaine, along with vitamin A, E, minerals, collagen concentrate, calf bone meal, lemon bioflavonoids, rutin, helperidan and herbs. After the first month of treatment, Winston complained about getting up only once. He now has a whole new gait. The "spring" is back in his step. The results were so immediate, the relief so obvious, that we started giving "Winston's Formula" to other dog owners with equally as dramatic results.*

*Winston has been on a one a day treatment for three months. Now we have cut back to a maintenance level of every other day or every third day. We will keep this up for the rest of his life. He will never by "cured", but from the look on his face, he certainly has "healed".*

-Mark Sherman, California


•**Tea Tree Oil** comes from many sources of trees. The most potent is extracted by steam distilling from the foliage of the melaleuca alternifolia from New South Wales. Some varieties are labeled organic, some are not. Tea Tree Oil has a high penetrating ability of skin and mucous membranes with a low incidence of skin sensitivity. It is antiseptic, antifungal, non-staining and can also serve as a mild local anesthetic. By stimulating blood flow, it can promote tissue and cell growth, healing a wound. It is useful on skin disorders, including ring worm, won't harm birds who peck at sores on their feet, helps heal cuts, fungus, saddle-sores, repels fleas and can be used to treat ear infections such as ear mites. Its strong smell disturbs some animals, such as cats, and should not be used where they could lick it off.

•**Vitamin C.** Although dogs and cats can manufacture ascorbic acid, the amount produced may not be sufficient to prevent or counteract stresses associated with injury, aging or joint malpositioning. Many animals cannot tolerate high levels of ordinary vitamin C, which can cause gastrointestinal distress. Ester-C contains calcium ascorbate which permits rapid absorption from the gastrointestinal tract. By reaching higher cellular levels it is being excreted more slowly than ordinary vitamin C and is well tolerated by cats, dogs and horses. A clinical study at Best Friends Animal Sanctuary was performed on dogs given this form of vitamin C. Animals on the Ester-C show marked improvement in mobility in musculoskeletal dysfunction's. This additional form of vitamin C is being used to treat animals with arthritis and mobility conditions.

## • FAT CATS (AND DOGS)

Excess fat is no small problem for animals. In fact obesity (15% higher than ideal body weight) is the most common form of malnutrition in dogs and cats. Pets are given too much food and too little exercise. The junk foods found on supermarket shelves do not promote optimum weight. Dry kibble may taste good, but too much of it may turn Tabby into a fat cat. Dog treats given in excess could also lead your pet to obesity. Fat animals are predisposed to diabetes, certain forms of cancer and a shortened life. Trying to put your pet on a diet may tax your patience listening to their whines and dealing with personality changes.

The new fad is "lite" pet foods which means low fat. Some of these may actually have more calories than the regular brands. Soon to be in effect, are new manufacturing requirements that detail specific caloric amounts for these diet foods. As we mentioned in *FATS in CHAPTER 1*, it is not the fats that contribute to obesity, but the type of fats. Do not be misled into purchasing low fat foods as a "cure" for your pet's paunch.

One of the latest useful treatments for overweight animals is (-) Hydroxycitric acid (HCA), an herbal extract of the fruit Garcinia species (trees common to parts of South Asia). HCA is a close relative of the citric acid found in oranges, lemons and other citrus fruits. A major pharmaceutical company found that the extract of Garcinia acts within the cells to block the production of fat from carbohydrate calories. Even when laboratory animals are given diets which were 70% sugar, researchers found that HCA reduced food consumption, body fat and blood lipid levels.

In Best Friends Animal Sanctuary in Utah, dogs fed maintenance diets supplemented with HCA and niacin-bound chromium showed an average weight loss of 8.6% below initial body weight without calorie restriction, exercise or changes in feeding frequency over a five week period. HCA works by inhibiting the enzyme that changes carbohydrate calories to fats. Another ingredient that shows promise in aiding weight loss is chromium. Scientists have found that when bound to niacin, chromium will boost the action of insulin, improve the body's ability to burn fat, synthesize body protein and inhibit breakdown of muscle tissue. Although applicability in animal nutrition has yet to be proven, chromium's beneficial effects have been shown in human studies.

Other fat burning nutrients are being studied. L. Carnitine, inositol and choline, herbs such as guarana, and minerals could boost fat burning in animals. Dietary substances that reduce appetite and body fat levels through natural physiological mechanisms, could tilt the odds of reaching "ideal" weights in favor of success and help dogs and cats enjoy the benefits of vitality and longevity with less risk of disease.

-contributed by L. Phillips Brown, D.V.M.


Dietary habit suggestions:
♦Feed pets less and more often.
♦Avoid junk food brands of commercial pet foods.
♦If food isn't eaten, remove it and offer it later.
♦Give natural supplements.  Pets are less likely to be hungry if their nutritional needs are satisfied..
♦Don't give treats as rewards...give love instead.
♦Increase exercise (play with your animals)
♦Provide plenty of pure water (to eliminate fats, waste, etc.)
♦Watch for behavioral changes and (or) healing crisis'
♦Monitor weight loss and don't put your pet on a crash diet.
♦Consult a veterinarian before starting any major weight loss program for your pet.
♦For underweight pets, don't go out and stock up on "bulk" foods such as cheap dry kibble. This may compromise their nutrition. Instead provide ample nutrients, high protein supplements, and minerals. By following many of the directions given in this book, you may find that if your pet is fed a normal quantity of premium food, they will fill out nicely. Thin pets may be nothing more than malnourished animals, even if they are eating their meals.

## • UNSUSPECTING HAZARDS (cat litter & vaccines)

*Litter*. Although this is not a nutrient, we include it because using the wrong litter, can definitely cause illness in your cat or ferret. Seventy-one percent of cat owners keep a litter box in their house. A majority of this is clay litter, which is not biodegradable and may cause sneezing and/or allergies in animals due to the dust created when they use it. Most of these litters do not cause anything more than an inconvenience as the animal tracks them around the house, but some can cause illness and even death. The biggest hazard to pet health from litter, is from the clumping varieties. Although convenient for disposal purposes, most clumping litter contains forty to one hundred percent of Sodium Bentonite as an agent, which swells to fifteen times its original size after absorbing moisture.

*When cats ingest or inhale this substance, this litter expands inside their body, forming a mass and coating its interior causing dehydration and preventing the absorption of nutrients or fluids. When it coats the digestive tract, it attracts the collection of old fecal matter, increasing toxicity, bacterial growth and prohibiting proper absorption of digested food. This can lead to stress on the immune system and promote illness including viral, bacterial, parasitic and yeast infections which may result in death. This agent acts as an expandable cement and therefore it should never be flushed down plumbing.* -Tiger Tribe, Nov. 1994 and Holistic Animal Care, 1994

Taking this statement one step further, it has been found in cats using this type of clumping litter, that their digestive tracts became plugged (just like plumbing) and they die because of blockage. There is an alternative type of clumping litter on the market that uses Guar as the clumping agent. It swells a minimal amount when it absorbs moisture and then begins to dissolve. Therefore it is able to pass through the digestive tract (and plumbing). One manufacturer only uses two percent of Guar in their litter, therefore it is considered safe. Please, for the life of your litter-bound pet, read labels carefully and do not use Sodium Bentonite based clumping litter.

Alternatives are cedar, recycled newspaper, corn, pelleted grasses, particulate wheat or plant fiber or wood fiber. A relatively new alternative to clay and clumping cat litter is environmental friendly, keeps dust down and avoids the aggravation of litter being tracked throughout the house. This litter is made from recycled newspapers and many times have natural additives that reduce odor from ammonia. It is a better choice than the clumping litter mentioned above, and clay litters, which can emit dust.

*Shots.* I was advised by a holistic vet, not to vaccinate my cat for feline leukemia this year, because studies have shown that trauma is caused at the site of the injections, many times leading to cancerous growths. He told me to keep her immune system strong with proper diet and nutrient supplements and most likely I wouldn't have to worry about this dreaded disease. I took his advice. People with pets whose immune systems are compromised and who aren't on a good nutrition regime, may not have been willing to take this risk.

Veterinarians agree that vaccinations can cause a variety of problems in animals, but they disagree as to the breadth and severity of their reactions. Illness contracted after shots were given, may not necessarily be related to the vaccination. Some breeds react more strongly than others to vaccinations, such as Rottweilers, Harlequin Great Danes, Akitas and Weimaraners. Many animals develop urinary tract infections after their annual shots, especially when more than one type is given during the procedure. Tumors developing at the site of the injection is another "side effect.." Since vaccinations are supposed to mimic the process of diseases causing the body to produce antibodies, minuscule amounts of the actual virus must be injected. This is unnatural.

Normally, infectious diseases travel a route through the body allowing the immune system to kick in at various stages. Injections bypass this normal routing and short circuit the very important primary response mechanisms. We have placed the virus directly into the blood and given it free and immediate access to the major immune organs and tissues without any obvious way of getting rid of it. Added to the assault are the many carriers added to the vaccine such as aluminum sulfate, mercuric oxide, formaldehyde, artificial colors, antibiotics, BHA and BHT or other chemicals. In real life, most animals will not experience attacks from multiple diseases at the same time as we give our pets during annual multi-shot treatments. Animals with weak immune systems will be at risk for either developing these diseases or contracting associated illness.

70

Many skin problems have been shown to develop from vaccinations as well as arthritic conditions and degenerative spinal diseases. Rabies vaccines are known to cause personality changes, skin changes, damage to the thyroid and endocrine systems, and lowered immunity. The side effects are not worth the risk if there are alternatives. Homeopathic nosodes, inactive virus essences, are now being used instead of vaccinations. They can be an effective alternative and have few side effects as they are more synergistic with the body but if an animal is immune compromised, they will still be subject to getting the disease which is true for vaccinations as well. An alternative as we mentioned before, is to fortify your pet's immune system through proper nutrition. Professional homeopaths also prescribe a single, specific remedy, based upon the totality of the individual symptoms to assist the defense mechanism in overcoming a developing disease. If given immediately after exposure to a known disease, nosodes can prevent the development of clinical disease and even the dreaded feline leukemia responds well to this type of treatment.

## EPILOGUE

We've provided you with a lot of food for thought and some pretty interesting stories. Hopefully, you will take most of this information to heart. Our kitties and pooches are victims of over zealous money hungry food manufacturers, chemical company opportunists and complacent pet owners. There are good people out there that are trying to give your pets a fighting change at a long and healthy life. We're cheering for them and so are your animals. Hopefully much of the information presented in this chapter has touched your heart enough to spark you to do more research. The resource directory at the end of this book lists companies that produce critter-friendly products. Write to them for more information. The smarter you get about your pet's health, the longer they will remain alive and healthy, as loving members of your family.


-Holistic magazine for pet owners: NATURAL PET Magazine, P.O. Box 420234, Palm Coast, FL 32142-0234 (904)-445-4608

## CHAPTER 3. FERRETS

A story came across the internet and spurred our interest in ferret health. We'll repeat it here and then continue on with this chapter. Although many people will not take the time or interest to prepare the mixture described below, Timmy's owner, Gary, proved that methods of nutritional healing can work. He recognized that commercial pet foods were not adequate for optimum ferret health, therefore he created his own. New advances in research, have brought us premium FERRET foods, available in the marketplace, that can contain most of the ingredients in Timmy's meal. With a proper diet we can eliminate many of the weaknesses that lead to illness. Adding supplements for immune support are always welcomed by the body and Gary's recommendations follow in line with information we have presented in this book.

→*"In early November, 1994, my ferret, Timmy was diagnosed with lymphoma. The prognosis was poor and they gave him two to three weeks to live. The lab also said it had spread to the liver, hepatic metastasis!! A friend said to give Timmy Gerber turkey rice, which I did along with an herbal tonic water. The vet prescribed liquid vitamins. I went to the All Pets Clinic after administering this regime, and they reported the lymphoma was eighty-five percent gone. Determined to fully cure Timmy, I tried Chinese herbs, homeopathy and acupuncture. The holistic vet also added coenzyme Q10. I developed a concoction to give him with a syringe (no needle), and I provided him with plenty of water in an herbal formula that had twenty-eight herbs and fruit extracts in it. One thing that really helped is my friend telling me to be aggressive in positive treatment with Timmy, not just grieve, thinking there's nothing we can do to help. Talk to him and tell him you love him and are glad he's alive. It seemed to really help.*

*The latest recipe I used to help Timmy totally recover is now shared daily by eight ferrets. Timmy eats about 70cc/day. I still feed him with a syringe if he boycotts his dish. Ingredients include: organic turkey vegetable baby food, lamb baby food; organic flax seed oil; nutritional yeast; powdered garlic; liquid vitamins; an herbal combination of red clover, burdock root, Oregon grape root, licorice and golden seal; adrenal support supplement; immune*

*support supplement; B complex in raisin juice; colloidal silver; clover honey; kelp; a green supplement containing spirulina, barley and alfalfa juice, chlorella, vitamin E, probiotics, royal jelly, bee pollen, herbs, green tea, grape seed extract and other anti-oxidants; Missing Link feline supplement with essential fatty acids, taurine, greens, garlic and other nutrients. My ferrets' energy levels are up overall, and Timmy is currently well, stable and absolutely beautiful."*
-Gary Holowicki, Colorado


## WHO IS A FERRET?

*Traus McWatters & Dancer*

Webster's dictionary defines a ferret as a kind of weasel, easily tamed and used for hunting rabbits, rats, etc. The domestic ferret is *not* a wild animal. It has been domesticated for three thousands years, which is longer than cats have been pets. Ferrets don't survive well on their own and no records have been found to indicate that ferret populations hang in your backyard as do feral cats and dogs. Ferret owners have developed their own terms forth their pets. Males are called hobs, females, jill, and youngsters are known as kits. Neutered males are known as gibs and females, sprites. Normally males weigh five pounds and females, three. Their lifespans average six to ten years....if fed properly. If you adopt a ferret, be prepared to interact with them a lot! They love to hide, get into everything, torment your dog or cat, and play all the time they are not sleeping.

*My roommate's ferret, Tinker, was relegated to wearing a bell so we could locate her when was out of her cage. She loved to play with our cats and they tolerated her for the most part. Unfortunately, she would jump on their back and hold on with her teeth firmly implanted in their neck. When she got over-zealous, she would chomp hard. We figured this must be how she killed prey in the wild. The cats figured this too, and at that point they would launch her across the room. She was a lovable creature, but we*

74

*definitely had to ferret-proof our house, just as a parent would have to do for a toddler. The alternative is to keep the animal in a cage. This is a sorrowful thing to do, as you can tell if you look at their pitiful little faces staring out of the bars. There should be a balance of indoor (in the cage), and outdoor (loose in the house) experiences for your ferret, if you want to maintain their sanity.* -Nina Anderson

Ferrets are not legal in two states because they are classified as wild animals although domestic ferrets are helpless in the wild and therefore should not be "set free". They also are feared to be a carrier of rabies, although the only member of the weasel family to have this problem is the skunk. Ferrets who contract rabies, die shortly thereafter, therefore the problem is solved by mother nature. If you plan to buy a ferret, please check out your state and local laws. You may need a license to keep them or it may be illegal to have them at all, with the consequences being their removal from your comfy home to meet a very uncertain fate.

## • FOOD

One of the best things you can do for your ferret, is to feed them a diet of fresh food. If you like to prepare your animal's dinner from scratch, there is a wonderful ferret diet available on the internet, (Pionus@ix.netcom.com). It includes 1/3 to 1/2 cup/day of raw ground turkey or chicken; Add to this 1 tsp. vegetarian mash (2 raw dandelion leaves, or 1/3 leaf of mustard greens, 1/3 lb. frozen corn, carrot, green beans, peas, 1/2 tsp. each cooked wheatberry/brown rice, 1/4 tsp. kelp granules/alfalfa powder); once or twice a week you can add a *tiny* bit of apple, banana and grapes.

People who do not want to play chef for their pets turn to canned or dry cat food. Cats and ferrets are different species and therefore have different nutritional needs. Tuna packed in salt water may be a yummy meal for Tabby, but it can cause salt poisoning in your ferret. There has been little research on ferret nutrition in the past, but that is changing because of the growing popularity of the animal. The domestic ferret is a meat eater, therefore should never be put on a vegetarian diet.

The ferret is a member of the family Mustelidae, carnivorous mammals that include skunks, mink and weasels. Although the size of a small cat, their intestines are about seventy-five percent the length of a cat, which makes their ability to process foods different from their feline friends. Since their large intestine is like a straight tube and lacks a ceacum (where most fiber digests), it is not very efficient at bacterial digestion or nutrient reabsorption. Food passes through an adult ferret in approximately three hours. Kits process foods in one to two hours. Therefore, offering foods that take five or six hours to digest, (like vegetables or foods with soy flour or corn gluten meal), will not be completely digested and therefore will do little good, nutritionally.

Because of this rapid digestion, ferrets should be fed many times a day or they become hypoglycemic and irritable. Pregnant jills that are off-feed late in the gestation period are susceptible to pregnancy toxemia, a life threatening condition. Also jills carrying large litters need *adequate* diets. If the mother becomes malnourished or doesn't eat regularly, her system can break down quickly making her weak and lethargic, have black tarry stools and shed her coat in handfuls. Without immediate medical attention, these animals will die. If a pregnant jill doesn't eat, you may want to try soft food such as warm baby food and make sure she gets nutritional supplements. One of the common reasons for not eating, is a change of food, therefore restrain from alternating your jill's diet until the kits have stopped nursing.

When kits become three weeks old, nursing mothers may lose weight. These jills and their kits can be offered a high calorie, high protein, palatable pelleted diet, softened with warm water. Although their eyes may not be open, the kits can still "smell out" the food. As the kits grow, ample water must be offered or they will restrict their intake of solid food, causing them to develop respiratory and intestinal ailments. Feeding them adequately will also prevent them from choosing your fingers as "food."

Ferrets, housed in areas accessible to natural sunlight, eat more in the fall, adding sometimes up to forty percent more to their weight. They instinctively reduce their intake of food in the spring and lose the weight, so don't worry too much. Obesity is not normally a problem, unless the ferret isn't allowed exercise and is fed lots of snack foods. The best way to put them on a diet, is to restrict their snacks, switch to a maintenance diet, and still continue to feed them many times a day as outlined earlier in this chapter.

76

PROTEIN & FAT.

Protein is required for tissue replacement, immune system maintenance, wound healing and stress. Since ferrets are carnivores, they require a diet high in *animal* based protein and fat. A diet based on plant protein, such as soy or corn, may lead to urinary tract infections because it causes too alkaline a pH in the urine. Also, plant proteins are not broken down and assimilated in the ferret's short gut. Animal proteins are more efficiently utilized. Since many commercial cat or dog foods and pelleted ferret foods are high in corn, wheat and soy, they are not the best choice for ferrets. Ferrets require at least ten essential amino acids which cannot be made in adequate quantities in the body and therefore must be obtained from food. Excellent sources of protein for the ferret are chicken, beef, eggs, liver, bone meal, and fish meal to a lesser extent.

Taurine, a lesser known amino acid is essential to cats and also thought to be for ferrets as well. It is only found in animal proteins such as poultry, beef, eggs, liver, and fish meal. Dry cat food contains approximately thirty percent protein. Ferret feed should contain thirty-five to thirty-eight percent protein for the average adult, therefore dry cat food is too low in protein for optimal nutrition. There has been some discussion on reducing the intake of protein for older ferrets.

Dr. Tom Willard, Ph.D. who has done extensive research on ferret nutrition, claims that reducing protein just because a ferret reaches a given age, is ill founded and potentially harmful to the ferret. He stresses, "the importance of considering the metabolizable energy of the diet, the ferret's "lifestyle," stress level and physiological stage of life for each animal. Since a ferret must be in positive protein balance, arbitrarily manipulating their diets could be disastrous. Only if the ferret has a *diagnosed* significant loss of kidney function, should you consider protein intake reduction." Vets may not be in agreement, but much of their advice may be based on research done with rats, many years ago.

Fat is needed by the ferret as a primary source of energy. Adult males should be fed food containing twenty-two percent fat; non breeding and older ferrets need at least eighteen percent fat. Animal fats are more digestible than vegetable oils and are added to many foods. Selected vegetable fats, found in many supplements, can provide a good supply of unsaturated essential fatty acids (Omega-3 and Omega-6) necessary to maintain supple skin and a thick, shiny coat.

Generally, both chicken fat and poultry fat are the highest quality source of fats, although fats from pork, beef as well as fish and vegetable oils may be combined to provide a balance of essential fatty acids. As mentioned in *HEALING FATS in CHAPTER 1*, essential fatty acids found in plant oils, are bioavailable to the body when in the complement of 'minor' nutrients, such as phytosterols, lecithin, vitamin E, and carotene. These maintain their nutrients if the manufacturer extracts them using cold extraction methods.

Oil supplements must be chosen carefully. Flax meal containing fiber, amino acids, and other nutrients for metabolism is a good choice and easy to mix into food. Flax and other meals should be used sparingly though, or they may cause loose stools. Bottled oils are excellent if they are cold extracted, organic, are in a dark bottle and have been kept away from light, which can promote rancidity once the bottle is opened. As a supplement, you can mix one tablespoon of flax oil with three ounces of evening primrose or safflower oil. Feed no more than four or five drops a day. Evening Primrose oil also contains GLA which older ferrets are less able to make. There are many supplements on the market which contain a full complement of essential fatty acids and many oils are provided with food exclusively made for ferrets.

→*"When Totally Ferret® came out on the market, I decided to try it. My __ferrets__ had been fed Iams Cat Chow since I began raising them. I did not have problems with that food, but I found that it did require supplementation with fatty acid products to prevent dry coats. I had tried to switch my ferrets to other foods over the years, but palatability was always a problem...they simply would not eat foods like Science Diet, Pro Plan, etc.*

*The ferrets readily accepted the new food without any mixing with the prior food and there were no bowel problems either. I immediately noticed a decrease in waste in the litter pans. In addition, after only two months on the food, I found that a ferret I had barely saved from __ECE (watery green diarrhea)__, who had been thin and very lethargic, began putting on weight and developed a healthy coat (after a year of barely hanging on to life). I have raised two litters on Totally Ferret® and neither jill developed hair loss*

*while nursing. The kits are exceptional in coat quality and size. I sold some kits to persons who had them on other types of food and it was impossible to recognize them as littermates of my kits. Their coats were dry and coarse, and they weighed much less than my kits. They had wonderful homes, but diet was the main variable. The owners have since switched to Totally Ferret® after seeing the brothers and sisters in my house!"*
-Diane Rogers, Pres. Baltimore, Maryland Ferret Club

CARBOHYDRATES.
Carbohydrates come in two types. The first, fiber (complex carbohydrates), is poorly digested by the ferret, but necessary to keep food moving through the digestive system and to keep the intestinal lining healthy. Since the ferret doesn't have a ceacum, digestive problems can arise if their diet contains three percent fiber or more, as found in most cat foods. Beet pulp is considered a good source of balanced fiber for the ferret, and when total fiber is found in concentrations of two percent or less, can allow good digestion and stool formation.

Starch, a specific type of simple carbohydrate is digestible in the ferrets if it is consumed *cooked* (soluble carbohydrates). This supplies metabolic energy which can substitute for some energy from fats and proteins. Simple carbohydrates are important in determining the texture of the food which makes it palatable to the ferret. Premium ferret foods are all fully cooked in a process where the starches are hydrated and heated to over two hundred degrees (to completely cook them). Foods that do not have the starches properly cooked are called pelleted foods. These are more difficult for the ferret to digest with the result being loose stools. Fully cooked (extruded) ferret foods are generally more palatable due to the expansion of the carbohydrates which make it crunchier.

• **MINERALS**

Minerals are involved in many enzyme systems which are involved in most of the body's metabolic processes. Macro minerals required in the greatest proportion in foods include calcium, phosphorous, sodium, potassium and chloride. Trace minerals (Micro minerals) include magnesium, zinc, iron, copper, manganese, iodine and selenium. Cobalt, chromium and sulfur are normally added to foods in a combined (organic), not pure form. The level of minerals is not as important as the balance, because too much or too little of a specific minerals can cause major problems and initiate many diseases.

In *MINERALS in CHAPTER 1*, we stress the importance of not supplementing your pet's diet with individual minerals. You are not a chemist and will not necessarily know how much is too much. You may want to consider having a hair analysis performed on your ferret to determine what mineral imbalances need to be addressed (see *RESOURCE DIRECTORY*). In most balanced foods, calcium should be from 1 1/4 to 1 2/3 times greater than the phosphorus level. If ratios are different from this, they can pose a problem for the animal. Sodium, potassium and chloride are important in maintaining proper fluid balance within the body. Ferrets small bodies are susceptible to dehydration, therefore it is important not only to provide the animals with plenty of fresh, pure water, but to make sure their mineral balance is adequate. The best way to supply minerals to your ferret, is to let the experts provide the proper complement in food or in supplements.

→*"Ever since I started incorporating Totally Ferret® into the ferrets diets, I have been amazed at the transitions. Some stray and neglected ferrets come in with thin and lackluster coats and physiques. After about two weeks on this improved diet, their coats shine, their skeletons flesh out, and they have more spirit and energy than when they arrived. Presently we have three week old kits who will be ready for mush in addition to mother's milk. Once again, Totally Ferret®, will be a part of the process to transition them through the weaning stage to a complete and balanced dry diet."*
-Pamela Grant, Director of The Ferrets of Pet Pals, Placement & Referral Service, Virginia (703)-354-5073

### • CHOOSING THE RIGHT FOOD

From the information we have provided you in this chapter, we hope you will now be aware that ferrets are different from cats and should not be given a constant diet of cat food. Many veterinarians will still recommend cat food, but please educate them. Cat foods are often too high in fiber (over 3%), and low in many essential vitamins and minerals needed by your ferret. Cat foods also contain corn and soy, which are poor quality ingredients for ferrets.

Normally pelleted ferret foods are modified mink foods. Usually, these have not been tested on ferrets, and you can identify them by their fishy smell. These foods are not adequate for ferrets either. You must learn to read labels and determine which is a premium ferret food. It should contain at least 36% protein, 22% fat and 2% fiber or less. The source of protein and fat considered to be excellent for the ferret are chicken, meat meal, whole eggs, liver, and herring meal. High quality simple carbohydrates such as rice flour or brewer's rice should be the second or third ingredient on the label. Fats from animal sources should be included with vegetable, flax or fish oils. Soy, wheat and corn proteins should never be fed to your ferret.

Remember that you must provide your ferret with dishes filled with fresh food so that they can munch on demand. Also make sure that their water bowls are always full. Dehydration can quickly send a ferret to their final resting place in the cosmos.

→ *" Early last November, I noticed my __ferret,__ Yoda was __losing body weight and mass__. He had been getting lighter a little at a time. On this particular morning when I picked him up, I was alarmed at how light he felt. In addition, he had been sleeping more and playing less. Being a subscriber to Modern Ferret Magazine, I began searching through past issues looking for places to call that might give me some idea as to what to do for Yoda. I called two companies from the ads, and asked if they could recommend anything for a geriatric ferret and both places said, "sorry, we can't help you." I was stunned, but persistent. The third call I made that morning was to the Totally Ferret® people.*

*Dr. Willard listened patiently to my request and asked questions as I explained my plight. He suggested that in addition to a visit to the vet, I might want to start Yoda on Totally Ferret®, and explained some things about ferret nutrition to me. He also gave me suggestions about how to transition him onto the new food. I followed his advice and gave Yoda the food he suggested. We watched him closely and within two weeks we saw a difference. The playful, exuberant, mischievous Yoda was back! In the two months that Yoda has been on Totally Ferret®, his activity level has increased, his coat is smoother than it has ever been and his weight has increased. Additionally, our four other ferrets are showing improvement in their coat quality as well, and one has even shown a dramatic improvement in behavior. (We previously called her "hell ferret".)*

-Judy Chenault,
North Carolina

TREATS.

Giving treats to your ferret can be one way of getting fresh foods into their diet. Packaged liver flavored cat treats are a good snack, occasionally. Vegetables such as shredded broccoli and chopped green pepper or chopped skinless cucumber are good choices as well as certain fruits like pears, and papaya. High fiber fruit such as raisins, bananas or apples are to be given only occasionally and in minute amounts, as ferrets have difficulty digesting them. Daily snacking on these sugary fruits has been associated with diabetes mellitus, an otherwise uncommon disease in ferrets. Crackers, puffed wheat, rice cakes or other grain products are not advisable as the grains do not digest well, and too much may cause diarrhea. Free-range cooked meat or chicken scraps are OK along with cooked egg scraps (never raw eggs). Sugar is definitely not to be part of the ferret diet and this includes chocolate, which is toxic to them. Other snack foods to avoid are dairy products, salty foods, bones, and foods with high levels of vegetable protein (soy, wheat gluten).

• **WATER, AIR AND LIGHT**

When you offer your ferret water, give them a sturdy dish. They drink more from bowls that water bottles. Because ferrets rest their front feet on the dish, make sure its heavy to prevent it from being tipped over. Your ferret doesn't have the choice of a babbling brook or dirty mud puddle to drink from. They depend on you to give them *clean* water. As we described in *WATER in CHAPTER 1*, tap water may not be a sound source of this life sustaining liquid. City water comes equipped with chlorine, fluoride, other chemicals and possible pathogens. Well water may contain pesticides and other ground water contaminants. Bottled water may be devoid of minerals making it "dead" water, giving no life force to the drinker. So what is your alternative?

Filtration is a good start. Either by installing a point-of-use filter or a whole house system, you can eliminate much of the contamination. Reverse osmosis, distillation and most bottled waters which have been filtered, provide clean water, but unfortunately the processing removes the good minerals along with the contaminants. Supplementing your supply with minerals will assure that your water retains its electrolyte base. There are liquid products on the market that can facilitate this process. As we have mentioned previously in this book, mineral supplementation is absolutely necessary because not only is the water mineral deficient, but the plants and animals are too. As the food chain progresses, our pets will feel the effects of this lack of minerals and their health will suffer. Many supplements listed in the *RESOURCE DIRECTORY* include minerals. Please contact the manufacturers for more information, as we cannot stress enough, the importance of adding minerals (in a balanced way) to your ferret's diet.

Minerals are basic to life. So is air. Indoor air can be contaminated and your ferret spends most of his or her life indoors, and they have no say in whether that air is kept fit to breathe. It is up to you to act as air quality controller in your homes. Airborne contaminants can trigger allergies in ferrets. Dust in kitty litters and environmental irritants such as pollen, smoke, perfume, household dust, chemicals outgassing from furnishings and cleaning products, and pesticides must all be considered.

These irritants remain in your house unless you open the windows. If you live in a closed environment (air tight), you should consider purchasing an air filtration or air purification unit. As we mentioned in *AIR in CHAPTER 1*, the health of your pet depends on your lifestyle. If you add chemically based decorating products to your home, clean with chemicals, smoke or even operate a gas appliance, the fumes will affect your pet. Add that to the dust and mold found in most houses, and your ferret will be hard pressed not to sneeze and have watery eyes. Air purification or filtration is absolutely essential to providing your pet a healthy place to live, and will also help to alleviate smells that they create, such as ammonia from urine. Air treatment devices are available everywhere, but they are not all alike. Contact the companies listed in the *RESOURCE DIRECTORY* for further information on eliminating your specific indoor air pollutants.

Ferrets too, can develop the seasonal affective disorder syndrome. If their cages are kept away from direct sunlight, you may want to supplement with full spectrum lighting as outlined in *LIGHT in CHAPTER 1*. Light is a nutrient, just like any of those we have covered in this chapter. It should be considered a part of any indoor animal's nutrition program. If your pet seems lethargic, depressed or irritable, you may suspect they are getting sick. It may be nothing more than lack of sunlight. Try placing their play area near a sunny window or put their harness on and take them for a walk outside. Repeated dosages of sunlight (from natural sources or full spectrum lights) may be all they need and save you a vet bill. Although this may be one solution, if it doesn't help within a short period of time, there may be another cause for the behavior change, in which case professional help may be necessary.

## • SUPPLEMENTS

•**Antioxidants.** Many ferret foods and most supplements contain vitamins C, E, A, the antioxidant vitamins. They fight infection and free radicals. They help prevent the oxygen damage that all eyes are exposed to and may have benefit in preventing cataracts. Vitamin C helps promote healing, is an immune strengthener and helps reduce arthritis pain. It works best when taken with vitamin E, one of nature's powerful antioxidants. Vitamin E found in the oil of the wheat germ, corn, sunflower and cottonseed, egg yolks and liver, is added to pet food to retard spoilage. Vitamin A supplements should be restricted to less than 1,000 IU daily because, unlike cats who are unable to convert Beta carotene to active vitamin A, ferrets do convert it, and therefore can cause build up to a toxic level.

•**Bee pollen.** It is richer in amino acids than any animal source containing five to seven times more amino acids than beef, eggs and cheese of equal weight. This is significant because the protein quality in most commercial pet foods is very low. Bee pollen is rich in nutrients and live enzymes, and high in lecithin, which is necessary for ferrets. Bee pollen helps increase brain functions, a plus for senior animals. It is a blood builder and strengthens fertility in breeding as well as combating allergies. It contains antioxidant vitamins A and E and therefore may control the runaway growth of cancer cells. Because of its vast range of nutrients, bee pollen is extremely beneficial for the immune system.

•**Blue-green algae** provides amino acids, minerals, enzymes, vitamins and chlorophyll. It is a good immune supporter and many pet owners have found its healing properties to be almost miraculous.

→*"One of the pets we own is a young __ferret__. On New Year's Eve, my husband and I went to the symphony. When we returned home, we found the ferret had gotten into a balloon topiary centerpiece on our coffee table. He must have had a ball, because every one of the ten or so balloons in that centerpiece was gone. After we spent awhile joking about the ferret enjoying his first New Year's Eve, we realized he may have eaten the balloons. We started to panic. We could find no remnants of broken balloons anywhere in the house.*

*I have a book written about ferrets by authorities that raise them for breeding. They state that the only recourse if the ferret __eats a foreign object__ (such as balloons), is surgery. Without this procedure, they will probably die. The balloons can create an impossible block in the intestines. Still yet, the ferret may die on the operating table as there is no definite formula as to how much anesthesia to give an animal weighing just a pound. My ferret was only about four and a half months old and not fully grown. I had to make a judgment call about the course of action to take.*

*He had been eating Super Blue Green™ Algae on his food since he became a part of our family at nine weeks old. Up until New Year's Eve, he had been very healthy. The first day after the incident, I increased the amount of Algae that the ferret was eating, and gave him Cell Tech's acidophilus on an empty stomach, first thing in the morning. He ate his morning breakfast at the appropriate time after eating the acidophilus and went right back to sleep. He slept until eight-thirty p.m. that evening. He had no bowel movement. The second day I continued the algae on his food. I did not find any bowel movements in his litter box. He slept until around five p.m. that day. The third day, the ferret woke up and relieved himself the first thing (which was his normal habit). Eureka! Red Christmas balloons!! I have continued to give the ferret anywhere from one-quarter to one-half a capsule of acidophilus every three to four days since January first and I still find red balloons coming out. I truly believe Cell Tech's products quite probably saved his life."*

-Sherry Swayze, Arizona Independant Distributor 117237

•**Calcium Ascorbate vitamin C.** Vitamin C has been shown to play a role in the immune system and as an antioxidant. Vitamin C, is rapidly excreted from the body, sometimes prior to its utilization. A more bioavailable form of this vitamin, calcium ascorbate, provides rapid absorption into the cells of the body. This form of vitamin C, Ester-C can help ferrets with respiratory problems and runny noses. One-twentieth of a teaspoon of Ester-C can help with mild sneezing or coughing. Be careful not to give them more than this or they may develop diarrhea. The best way to administer it, is by putting one teaspoon of powdered Ester-C in one ounce of fruit juice and give seven drops three times a day. Ester-C is also helpful in the beginning, if your ferret gets distemper, although most animals die from this disease eventually.

•**Cat's Claw (Una de Gato)** active constituents, oindole alkaloids, have been proven to increase the ability of the white blood cells and macrophages to attack and digest abnormal cells, harmful microorganisms and toxic matter. Cat's Claw contains numerous plant substances that have tremendous antioxidant properties more powerful than vitamin E and C.

•**Flax** is a superb source of Omega 3 essential fatty acids. These essential fatty acids contribute to a lustrous coat, eliminate bald spots, help prevent dry skin and heal red and raw areas. Flax oil or flax meal are excellent sources of these life enhancing nutrients. Read *HEALING FATS in CHAPTER 1.*

•**Lecithin** is a fat burner and promotes alertness as well as steadying the nerves.

•**Natural care products.** Not all shampoos are good for animals, especially those with chemicals in them. Better for your ferret are those having nutritional ingredients such as aloe, jojoba oil or herbs.

86

•**Nutritional (Bakers') yeast.** Primary (not Brewer's) yeast is a high source of B vitamins (thiamin, riboflavin, niacin, pyridoxine, Pantothenic acid, biotin and folic acid), amino acids (lysine and tryptophan which are deficient in grains), and minerals (including molybdenum, chromium and selenium which are deficient in most diets). Nutritional yeast promotes hair growth, helps in repelling fleas, and supports the immune system. Baker's yeast is preferred over Brewer's yeast because it is grown under carefully controlled conditions, on purified mixtures of cane and beet molasses. This allows nutritional uniformity and produces higher levels of B vitamins. Brewer's yeast is a by-product of the brewing industry obtained from sediment left over after fermentation. It is harvested after fermenting as many as ten or eleven batches of beer and may contain a number of unknown yeast types, some not so healthy.

•**Oxygen Enhancers** are useful, especially for animals who exert themselves, such as racing dogs or horses. Adding oxygen supplements to your pet's diet helps enhance nutrient absorption and can be a powerful respiratory aid.

•**Probiotics** are found naturally in the gastrointestinal tract of healthy animals.These microorganisms provide "friendly" bacteria in the colon to assist with digestion, elimination are restoration of proper flora balance after upset or illness. Environmental, nutritional or situational changes can disrupt and decrease these beneficial micro-organisms in the digestive tract. Without the good bacteria, harmful strains can take over causing intestinal problems. Supplementation may be necessary, especially after usage of drugs, such as antibiotics, which kill beneficial flora.

•**Royal Jelly** is the white milky substance produced by worker bees, that feed the queen and increase her size sixty percent. Royal jelly contains taurine, an essential nutrient for ferrets. Royal jelly can help with arthritic conditions, better coats, relief from insomnia, increased energy and a speedy recovery after surgery.

•**Spriulina.** This planktonic blue-green algae is a good source of amino acid and vitamin B-12 and is different from most algae in that it is easily digested. Scientific studies show that spirulina strengthens the immune system, causes regression and inhibition of cancers as well as inhibiting viral replication by preventing cell penetration by the virus. It is then rendered harmless by the body's defense system. It is also high in GLA essential fatty acid, stimulating growth in

animals and making skin and coat shiny and soft. It feeds the
beneficial intestinal flora and is excellent in alleviating symptoms of
arthritis. Spirulina is also good at treating parasitic or bacterial
infections.

•**Tea Tree Oil** has a high penetrating ability of skin and mucous
membranes with a low incidence of skin sensitivity. It is antiseptic,
antifungal, non-staining and can also serve as a mild local anesthetic.
By stimulating blood flow, it can promote tissue and cell growth,
healing a wound. Its strong smell disturbs some animals, such as cats,
and should not be used where they could lick it off. Tea Tree Oil is
effective for ear mites in ferrets.  place a single drop in each ear daily
for one week, rest one week, then repeat for another week.

## EPILOGUE. TIPS FOR FERRET HEALTH.

♦Ferret proof your house to prevent them from eating non-digestible
items such as rubber, cotton, wood, plastic, styrofoam.  Unable to
pass these substances, ferrets can die unless drastic procedures are
taken by your veterinarian..

♦Choose ferret toys carefully so they don't ingest substances as
stated above.

♦Always use a harness while taking a ferret for a walk outside.
Domestic ferrets are not wild animals and will not survive well if they
run away.

♦Avoid plastic aquariums for ferret homes.  They outgas fumes that
can be harmful to your pet's health.

♦Keep your home cool in the summer.  Ferret's don't tolerate heat
well if over 80 degrees.  In winter, give them a snugly place to sleep
so they'll stay warm.

♦Beware of vaccinations. See the section, *UNSUSPECTING
HAZARDS in CHAPTER 2*. Similar concerns for vaccines are
addressed for ferrets as well as cats and dogs. If you are giving your
ferret a distemper shot, it should be for canine distemper, not feline.

♦Avoid clumping litter with Sodium Bentonite as an agent, which
swells to fifteen times its original size after absorbing moisture.  This
type of litter can have devastating effects on the health of your ferret.
Use alternatives as we have outlined in *UNSUSPECTING HAZARDS
in CHAPTER 2*.

♦Play with your ferret.  Animals kept caged will develop depression,
neurotic behavior and health problems associated with inactivity.

Besides, you'll miss the very reason to have a ferret. Their humorous antics and the love they can share.

-Magazines for ferret owners: MODERN FERRET, by Crunchy Concepts Inc., PO Box 338, Massapequa Park, NY 11762 (516)-799-1364; FERRETS, USA , Fancy Publications, 3 Burroughs, Irvine, CA 90057 (714)-855-8822

-Neat book...from Carlton Press: *The Fairfax Ferret* by Pamela Grant, about a boy, allergic to cats, who discovers ferrets make the perfect pet.

-North American Ferret Assn. P.O. Box 1963, Dale City, VA 22193

-American Ferret Assn., P.O. Box 3986, Frederick, MD 21705-3986, phone (888)-FERRET-1

## CHAPTER 4. HORSES

Veterinarians diagnose a host of ailments in horses from skin conditions, colic, and bone disease, to behavior disorders and depression. Most problems in horses are related to dietary insufficiencies or imbalances. Almost every horse owner at one time or another, has seen their animal chewing on fence posts. This may be due to a dietary deficiency and your horse may be trying to tell you something. Horses know lots of things we don't! They instinctively seek out acid plants if their bodies are too alkaline. They look for specific herbs to heal their illness and they will vary their feed accordingly. Of course, this depends on a free-choice environment which wild horses enjoy. (I wish we could be as tuned in to our bodies as they are to theirs!)

Captive animals depend on humans and even though we try to do what is right, we may not always fulfill their dietary needs. Every horse owner has their own ideas about nourishing their animals, but many times they receive their information from the feed store or manufacturer advertising. They may not always have your horse's best interest at heart, especially when it comes to providing balance in a diet. We will offer you information, some of which you may be familiar with, some which may be new. As with any dietary program we advise that if you decide to change your feeding habits, do so gradually as abrupt switches in feed can send your horse's digestive system into shock. A breeder's story outlines a remarkable success with diet and gives hints to applications for certain ailments

→*"As a breeder and professional "foaling midwife" for twenty years, we have seen our share of abnormal births and orphan foals. This year we foaled our first set of live **twin thoroughbred foals**. To be alive was a good sign, but to be sound in lung, bowel and limb was a miracle!*

*To insure that this miracle progressed properly, we put the "boys" on fresh goat's milk free-choice, along with free-choice nursing. By the time the colts reached two months, they were consuming up to two and one half gallons of goat's milk a day, plus a couple of pounds of a twelve percent sweet feed pellet mixture, and 12-12 Purina mineral with HorsePhos and Clovite added in. By three and one-half months, they were weaned off the milk and the grain was increased to four pounds daily. They are now six months old, growing up very, very nicely, conformation and size wise. The mare, who normally at weaning time loses a lot of weight, is fat and shiny. We have high hopes for our "boys" and so far, they are progressing nicely.*

*Sunset Meadow Farm twin foals*

*Most of our applications for treatments are holistic in nature and many stem from folk remedies. A few of my recipes for sick horses are listed below:*

*-For horses who tie-up after exercise and show extreme pain, stiffness, rapid pulse and brown urine, I find remarkable improvement when given two tablespoons of Epsom Salt two times daily in their feed.*

*-For horses with sore throats due to allergies, dust, hay, etc., I dose them a few times daily by oral syringe with a mixture of honey, apple cider vinegar, water and chamomile tea. They even like the taste!*

*-Washing a horse with white vinegar and water can help keep the flies away.*

*-Yogurt is a wonderful way to settle minor stomach ills and is a help with ulcer treatments."*

-Jeanne Vuyosevich, Sunset Meadow Farm, New Jersey

## • FEED

There is a general misconception about the feeding of stable horses. A little, hay, a little grain, sometimes an apple and ala! a healthy horse. Maybe, maybe not. Much research has gone into diets for indoor pets and feed lot animals, but very little money has been spent on equine nutrition. Wild horses are foraging animals, grazing on natural grasses, eating constantly and seeking out just those specific herbs that will help any illness they happen to think they have.

Domestic horses, on the other hand, are fed when it's convenient for the stable person, and given a diet for which they normally have no choice. They are made to do certain tasks, like pulling and supporting a rider, that the wild horse never has to encounter. It's no wonder that the domestic horse has an increase in chronic disease. Normally this animal doesn't develop illness' common to household pets such as cancer, heart disease, liver and kidney disorders. The horse's ailments focus in the area of the digestive and respiratory tracts, skin and hooves, eyes, muscles and they even have behavior disorders.

Horses have different digestive systems than dogs and cats and are more susceptible to inadequate diets. Their acid stomach digests protein, while their small intestine digests the fat and carbohydrates. The most important part of a horse's digestive system is the cecum, where the digestion of fiber takes place. The cecum must be kept full, because if it is partly empty, there will be a gap in the intestinal tract which could twist. This condition leads to colic, which sometimes is fatal. Since the cecum digests long stem fiber, if the horse's diet is deficient in this type of feed, they will be predisposed to digestive problems. Also, if the horse is only fed twice a day, and stands idle in a stall, the cecum will again become void and potentially cause a problem.

## CARBOHYDRATES & FATS.

Horses need carbohydrates and fats to maintain their energy levels, and since they are not meat eaters, they must get these from other sources. Carbohydrates make up sixty percent of most grains and hays and become the "fuel" for maintaining body functions such as heart, respiratory and temperature regulation. Fats are most abundant in corn and oats which supply twice as much heat and energy as carbohydrates. They also help in vitamin A and calcium absorption. Fats also contribute a higher amount of water from metabolism than carbohydrates and proteins. This is important for endurance horses because it helps prevent dehydration when they sweat. Fats can be efficiently utilized for slow, low intensity exercise,

However, it has been shown that thoroughbreds improve their race times when consuming a diet containing twelve percent of its feed being oil, rather than fat obtained from grain.

Fats obtained by the addition of oils to your horse's diet, need to be guarded against spoilage. Preservatives added to feed, have most commonly been in chemical form. Investigate feed companies using more natural preservatives like vitamin E, C or A. If you choose to add oils to the feed, buy cold extracted oils. Cold pressing keeps the nutrients in tact and is healthier than heat extraction methods which can produce carcinogens. Corn, sunflower, canola and safflower oils are most commonly added to feed. Oils supply two and one half times more calories than grain, and are used to up the horse's energy intake for the same amount of food. It has been reported that a horse is capable of digesting and utilizing up to thirty percent of his energy need as fat, without developing digestive problems.

In order to accomplish a safe increase in a fat diet, the oils should be introduced slowly so that the digestive and metabolic systems can adjust. Vitamin E and selenium must be increased when adding oils to the diet. Vitamin E prevents oxidation of fats to peroxides in muscle cell walls and blood. Peroxides can reduce the efficiency of muscle function and overall performance. Selenium also prevents oxidation and protects against muscle damage, irritation and inflammation. (Rule of thumb is to add 100 IU of Vitamin E per 3 1/2 ounce of added oil.) Essential fatty acids (EFA's), necessary for good coat and skin conditions are abundant in oils. For a complete description of EFA's read *HEALING FATS in CHAPTER 1.*

→*"We bought our new **horse** in January of 1995 and our trainer got us started on Missing Link, whole food supplement. After a couple of weeks, we could see the difference in Oliver's **coat**. He is very thin skinned and doesn't like to be brushed a lot. We were surprised to see dapples coming out on his neck and hind quarters. People were coming up to us at shows and commenting on how shiny and beautiful his coat was. This winter, when everyone else had to shave their horse, Oliver's coat was still short and shiny. While on this product, my daughter and Oliver came home with some impressive show results: Four firsts, Children's Hunter Champion in Coto De Caza show, Feb. 1995; Four firsts in different categories in Ride America, March 1995 and first at the*

*Interscholastic Equestrian League show in March, 1995. Six firsts in the O.C.H.S.A. Championship Show and many more."*
-Julie Froley, California


→*"I have been training __horses__ professionally for the past thirty years, and one of my first priorities is a balanced feed program. Over the years, I have been given many free samples of supplements and I have won in competition, many more. I've even been asked to endorse products I hadn't even used. Needless to say, I have become adverse to any new supplement to come out on the market. However, last January, I became very interested in The Missing Link whole foods supplement, after being informed that it was originally designed for small animals, and I had used it for my dog, first.*

*I anxiously tried it on one __horse__ that had always jumped beautifully even though he __didn't jog sound__. After two weeks on The Missing Link, he was sound and has been ever since. In addition, as an unexpected surprise, this horse had a major disposition change. He had always been a __suspicious and nervous__ type. His attitude changed so much that everyone in the barn noticed. In April, I decided to put every horse, in my care, all forty-five, on The Missing Link. Horses I've been battling nervousness with for years have changed attitudes with little or no extra work. The amount of anti-inflammatory distributed to the horses in my barn has decreased to less than half, as well as leg bandaging. Hoof and coat condition has improved drastically. Horses have come out of retirement and are jumping at shows again, including well known horses like "Capital Gains" and "Backfire." I used to stock the shelves with at least ten different vitamins, minerals and oils. Now I just use this one."*
-Larry Mayfield, California


## PROTEIN.

Protein is needed to maintain a horse's vital organs and especially for good physical development of young horses. Twenty kinds of amino acids must be present for proper assimilation of protein by the horse, and many grains don't provide this full complement. Normal plants used for their protein are alfalfa, hay, linseed (from flax), cottonseed and soybean meal (source of the most protein). Never use *raw* linseed oil, as it contains a poison that is

95

removed when boiled. Soy has also been known to be toxic to horses because the solvents used in processing this bean, prevents it from being completely digested, creating problems in the intestines. The best natural source of protein is from alfalfa,.

According to the National Research council., adult horses of all breeds require only 7.5 to 12 percent protein. The lowest percent of protein in commercial feed available today is ten percent and sometimes run as high as sixteen percent, therefore horses may be getting excess protein in their diets. Too much protein throws the digestive system out of balance, potentially resulting in ulcers, mastitis, joint disorders in foals, liver and kidney problems, soft feet, poor hair coat and behavior disorders. Race or show horses need more protein, but since they normally eat more grain, their protein needs should be satisfied.

Concentrates of protein sources normally come in pellets, whole, cracked or steamed forms. If you purchase ready made feeds, read the label to make sure the level of protein is not excessive. Pelletized food must be given with lots of water because they are dry and will contribute to dehydration. One pound per day *only*, is usually recommended. Feeding pellets will help put bulk on a horse who doesn't have much access to grazing, but has adequate hay.

Corn, barley and oat based grain mixtures also provide protein, but balancing these grains in the right amount can be difficult. Veterinarians claim that most problems stem from the excess use of grains which are low in calcium and high in phosphorus, and they have seen a lot of bone problems in animals who are fed a high grain, low hay diet. They also have seen orthopedic disease in foals due to overfeeding and excess use of energy foods such as grain. Most claim that it should never make up more than half of the diet. Measuring is the key to avoiding excesses and not all grains measure out the same way, for instance a one quart coffee can holds two pounds of oats and sweet feeds, but three pounds of barley, and slightly over three pounds of corn or whole wheat. Feeding grains also depends on the horse's preference. They may stick their nose up at one type and gobble up another.

If corn is given, use the flaked type of feed, as this is more easily digested. Cracked corn is digestible too, but some of the proteins may be removed during processing. Corn has the lowest heat of digestion of any grain (because of its low fiber content) and is an excellent choice for endurance horses. Corn on the cob is a treat for horses, but be advised that some horses may choke on the cob if they don't chew properly.

Oats have a high energy content, but they must not be stored for more than three weeks after rolling or they lose much of their nutritive value. Oats shouldn't be given whole as they are hard to digest in that form. Crimped, rolled or cracked oats are better. Barley is a great energy food for horses and is less irritating to their digestive system, but since it is more concentrated, you must feed them less.

Be discriminating in selecting feed companies. Ask questions! Many of them use floor sweepings and dust in their "recipes." They use molasses to sweeten the grain and since molasses is a sugar, it can create hyperactive animals. Molasses is also preserved with propylene glycol (*see FOOD in CHAPTER 2*), that can create allergic reactions in all animals, including horses. Pelleted feeds do not normally include sweeteners, therefore they are an alternative choice. *Caution:* some horses bolt their food and may choke on pelleted feed. One solution is to put a large rock or a brick in their feed tub to slow them down. Also, feeding small meals many times a day, and wetting their food may reduce the problem.

GRASSES.

Pasturing horses is one of the nicest things you can do for them. Not only are they happy to be free, but they can munch on a fresh source of feed. Bluegrass, brome, timothy, prairie grass, and fescue are some good choices for grass. Hays vary depending on which part of the country you live in. Timothy grows up north, wheat grass in the west, Bermuda grass in the south and orchard grass in the middle of the country. Planting pastures of legumes such as clover, alfalfa and espedeza are a great complement, but are too rich to use as the primary diet. For instance, too much alfalfa can give them soft stools and lead to colic. Horses need seventy-five percent grass to twenty-five percent legumes. For animals kept indoors during the winter, reintroduce them to lush pastures slowly (a few hours at a time), so they won't be able to gorge themselves and develop colic.

Hay forms the bulk of a horse's diet, especially if they are stabled for most of the year. Hay should be given *long*, not chopped up, as the cecum needs the long-stem fiber for digestion. A horse is meant to eat long stem fiber for twenty hours a day, not a few quick meals of just hay. Alfalfa hay is good as long as the measured protein content is around twelve percent (some alfalfa hay measures twenty-two percent which is too high for horses). A variety of grasses is best, combined in proper balance with legumes.

Giving your horse baled hay requires its own set of rules. Horses can develop allergies to mold, therefore it is imperative to dry the hay before baling. Cutting it before it turns to seed will assure the hay will keep most of its nutrients and shaking out hay rations will help eliminate dust and foreign objects. Beware of giving horses fresh hay as this can cause colic. Wet or moldy hay can kill a horse, cause fungal infections and in allergic animals, lung infections. Oats and concentrates of feed also must be dust and mold free, to prevent allergic reactions. Silage, useful as a substitute for horses with mold allergies, has been used as feed, but it makes their droppings loose 'Big bale' silage is not to be used, as soil contaminants can result in botulism poisoning.

## • NUTRITIONAL DEMANDS ON THE ENDURANCE HORSE

The information for this section, has been graciously provided by James Helfter of Advanced Biological Concepts. James is dedicated to providing animals and birds with the best nutrition possible. The idea for all natural feed additives came to Mr. Helfter years ago after retiring from aerospace research and development. He says, "our society believes the only way to fix disease is through poison. I believe we have an alternative."

"Unexplained metabolic failures are often due to nutritional imbalances. Having your horse nutritionally balanced prior to competition is more critical than what you feed during competition. In thinking nutritional balance, one must consider both *excesses* and *deficiencies*. An excess of nutrients will overload the elimination organs, liver and kidneys, these being very important organs to an endurance horse. To have good liver and kidney function, it is critical to not overload them by nutrient excesses and chemicals. Many feed supplements are imbalanced with excesses of the cheaper nutrients and deficiencies of the more expensive ones.

Electrolyte balance is your next consideration. It is critical that electrolyte balance be reached at the cellular level prior to any competition. Utilizing an electrolyte that is *balanced* and *available* is essential. The horse's digestive tract must be healthy and the rest of his diet needs to be balanced or the electrolytes will not be properly absorbed. Electrolyte demand is dependent upon a number of factors: trail condition, temperature, humidity, elevation and the condition of your horse. The quantity of electrolytes required is not completely understood, and published recommendations may not take into account the increase in metabolic rate that occurs with endurance riding. Observe your horse when giving electrolytes. If they constantly reject your electrolyte, re-appraise the product that you are using. Some electrolytes can upset the stomach and suppress the appetite. There is an advantage to pre-loading with electrolytes the night before and morning of a race.

The majority of horses are fed wet feed during a competition, but there can be drawbacks to feeding wet feed. If a horse drinks his fill of water and then is offered wet feed, he may limit the intake of the wet feed and consequently limit his intake of calories. A highly palatable and calorie condensed dry feed needs to be made available. Horses also need to be acclimated to wet feed ingredients. This would require feeding your wet feed ingredients, at least once a day to maintain the digestive enzymes in the intestine needed for proper digestion of those ingredients. In warm weather, when wet feed is mixed up and sits around waiting for the horse to arrive at a checkpoint, fermentation can begin immediately with no warning. This may upset a horse's digestive tract.

Wheat bran is often used as an ingredient in wet feeds. Wheat bran, however, has an extreme calcium and phosphorus imbalance which makes it an unsound nutritional ingredient. Some schools of thought feel that feeding bran mash on a regular basis is like giving your horse a laxative. It may be useful to keep things moving along in the intestinal tract so food doesn't settle and form blockages, but it also may give a false sense of proper bowel movement, thereby masking a problem. If you are trying to add water to the feed, beet pulp is a superior product and it has other nutritional benefits. When soaking beet pulp, consider adding electrolytes to the water. This yields a time-release mechanism for electrolytes and water.

Water is the number one nutrient to be considered during a competition. The consumption of water for an average horse is three pounds of good quality water per each pound of feed ingested. Additional water intake beyond this, is a must for an endurance horse during a competition, both for cooling purposes and maintaining proper hydration. Ideally, the water that his digestive tract is accustomed to at home, would be the water of choice prior to and during a competition. (Often not very practical.) Always remember, if your horse chooses to drink water from mud puddles, etc., which seems to you not very wise or palatable, please trust him as he definitely knows what he needs to continue at the current work load.

I would like to encourage you to offer your horse different choices during the ride, to find out what he prefers when he is working hard. For instance, offer wet and dry feed, grass hay and alfalfa hay, as well as free choice vitamins, minerals, and salt. During a competition, horses have very individual requirements.

Alfalfa hay is very high in calcium and low in phosphorus. Because of this imbalance, it should be avoided in your horse's daily ration. Horses normally take calcium from their bones to replace calcium lost in sweat. If they are fed alfalfa hay before a ride, the calcium shift from the bones to the blood is inhibited. If your only option is utilizing alfalfa hay in the daily ration of your horse, withhold alfalfa hay eighty-four hours prior to competition and re-introduce it twelve hours before to assure maximum calcium absorption capabilities during the competition.

Microflora, enzymes and special food for the gut bacteria have proven very beneficial for endurance horses to maintain gut sounds and appetite during competition. A high protein diet has no place for most endurance horses. They are not meat production animals and we are not looking for muscle bound athletes. High protein diets are also detrimental to liver and kidney function. Soybean meal is the most common source of protein in a packaged feed. It is an imbalanced protein source and thus not a wise choice for an endurance horse.

The molasses found in feed usually contains propylene glycol and chemical preservatives. (see *FOOD in CHAPTER 2.)* Both of these ingredients have detrimental effects on the digestive tract micro flora and to the liver and kidneys. Generally, sweet feeds need to be avoided for endurance horses. De-worming programs should be evaluated. De-wormers are extremely hard on horses and should only be used after fecal samples have indicated the need for a de-wormer. Only the mildest de-wormer should be used, and horses should never be de-wormed closer than fourteen days prior to a competition in order to preserve intestinal health.

The best advice we can give you is to experiment. The greatest technological advances can be gained by observing your horse during competitions. Discover what he will eat and go from there to find the winning combination. Remember, your horse is special and has special needs. Always keep in mind: To **Finish** Is To Win."
-James Helfter

## • MINERALS

It was once thought that a horse grazing on open pastures and drinking from streams, received sufficient minerals. That scenario is no applicable today. Modern farming methods have depleted soils of minerals and when they try to add them back, they don't fertilize with a full complement, further unbalancing the soil. Acid rain further complicates the process. It lowers the soil pH, typing up certain nutrients and making them unavailable to plants. Compounding the problems is the fact that the plant, hungry for minerals, starts taking up aluminum and other heavy metals out of the soil. Animals eating these plants can ingest the wrong kind of minerals, which may lead to disease. (see *MINERALS in CHAPTER !.*)

Many horses may have subclinical nutrient deficiencies that prevent them from reaching their maximum potential. Mineral deficiencies can cause a host of problems. For example, if selenium is missing in the diet, foals cannot grow properly and adult horses suffer from sore muscle problems. Horses will select from free-choice minerals as long as they are not too sick. For instance, when winter approaches, horses will select sulphur sources. They must know that sulphur assists in the production of hair, necessary to add thick winter coats.

The skeleton of a horse weighs over one hundred pounds, fifty of that which is made up of minerals, mostly calcium and phosphorus. These minerals must be balanced in a ratio of one and a half to two parts calcium to one part phosphorus. If too much phosphorus is present the horse may develop osteomalicia, which can be treated by re-balancing these minerals. Calcium supplementation can come from steamed bone meal or decalcium phosphate. Other minerals needed are iodine, cobalt, manganese, copper, iron, molybdenum, selenium and zinc. Chromium is needed in carbohydrate and fat metabolism.

When researchers at Kentucky Equine Research added supplemental chromium to the diets of well-conditioned horses, they found the animals had lower plasma cortisol and lactate levels in their blood after exercise, indicating this group was less stressed by exercise than the control group. Researchers at Texas A&M University found that feeding supplemental silicon to weanlings increased their radiographically-measured bone density. They also found fewer exertion-induced bone injuries and faster race times in young horses fed silicon.

Supplementing with trace minerals is essential. They can be added to salt blocks or feed or if in liquid form, can easily be added to their water. Feeding your horse minerals through a salt block alone is not the answer. Since these are ninety-five percent salt, if a horse doesn't feel it needs salt, they won't lick the block. Excess salt will also limit the uptake of other essential minerals, therefore a salt block should not be given at the same time a trace-mineral supplement is offered. The advantage of adding mineral supplements to a horses diet is evidenced by the following story.

→*"A test was conducted at Finger Lakes **race** track in upstate New York, using five subject **horses** from the stable of trainer, Mr. David Traus, and completely overseen by the track veterinarian, Mr. Frank Loparco. A liquid mineral supplement Pet-Lyte™ was administered orally, morning and night each day, through a dose syringe at full strength.*

*After the third day there was a noticeable increase in their intake of water, which by the end of the testing period had doubled from what the horses had consumed prior to the start of testing. After the fifth day, the **muscle soreness** seemed to be disappearing and the horses were much more alert, and less **nervous and jumpy**. By the seventh day, one horse with a history of **low hemoglobin** which consistently tested in the 11.8 to 12.2 range, was up to 13.85.*

*After the twelfth day, there was a distinct difference in their coats as they started to dapple out and become shiny. One horse with a two year old bare patch of skin from a prior injury, even began to grow back his hair.*

*By the end of two weeks, muscle soreness had completely disappeared and perhaps most impressive, all the horses raced excellently. Not only did they win three out of five starts, with one second, but more importantly, after the races, there was no soreness of stiffness detected. One horse, A Blooming Miracle, beaten by some eleven lengths prior to being put on Pet-Lyte ™ came back with two straight wins over the same company of horses after taking the mineral supplement. Mr. Loparco was so impressed with the equine formula, he began taking the human formula, Trace-Lyte ™. Pet-Lyte is used by the DuPont stables, with similar results, and it has taken until this time to develop the formula so that it would stay suspended in solution for mass production. "*

-Dr. I. (Gerald) Olarsch, N.D., North Port, FL

Supplementing a horse's diet with minerals can not only keep adults sound, but assure that foals develop strong bones as well. Giving the wrong balance of minerals could get your horse into trouble. Young horses can easily get an imbalance of calcium and phosphorus that can lead to improper growth. Normal procedures for this, ask for injections of vitamin D and calcium. If a horse is being fed alfalfa which is high in calcium, the addition of a calcium supplement may create an excess. Race horses have a lot of bone problems and need calcium *in the right balance*. Too much iron will tie up calcium. Low levels of phosphorus can prevent the bioavailability of calcium. So you see by playing mineral wizardry with your horse, you may be doing more harm then good.

Taking a "whole body" approach is wiser and giving a mineral supplement with the proper complement of trace elements will assure maximum absorption of the necessary minerals. Complementary nutrients may also act to strengthen a mineral's job. Silica, when taken with calcium has been proved to provide stronger and more flexible bones. Boron can act as a carrier for calcium. The body works in synergy and each nutrient works in and for the support of another.

To be absorbed into a horse's system, minerals must be bioavailable. Chelated and crystalloid forms of minerals fit into this category. Chelation means the mineral is hooked to amino acids that help them get across the gut wall more easily. Seaweed, a viable supplement, contains over sixty known trace minerals, twenty vitamins, plus amino acids and fatty acids  Crystalloid means minerals have been reduced in size so they permeate the cell wall.  Crystalloid minerals are found in liquid form and with electrolytes, balance to support the horses system..

Don't expect instant results when supplementing with minerals. Deficiencies that took a long time to build cannot immediately disappear. Still, many letters to manufacturers report dramatic changes in only a matter of weeks after mineral supplementation. Minerals aren't the only problem with feed but can offer a level of protection for your horse. Chemicals, preservatives and pesticides are big culprits. Modern agriculture dictates that the best grains go to humans and leftovers to horses, just as by-products fill dog and cat food cans. A Rutgers University study on nutrition showed eighty-seven percent less minerals and trace elements in commercially versus organically grown vegetables (grain and hay are no different!). Non-organic fertilizers make hay and grain look good, but they don't necessarily nourish this feed. Pesticides used in bug control find their way into the grain and therefore into your horse's body where they can cause long term disease, including tumors.

Cells of the body are equipped to remove waste and toxins, nourish themselves to regenerate and build healthy new cells if they receive the proper raw material. Chemical fertilizers and pesticides interfere with this process. Minerals can be of assistance as they facilitate the chelation of metals and certain toxins out of the blood, protecting the animal somewhat from this chemical assault. If minerals are in short supply, these toxins will have a negative effect on the health of your horse. The most wholesome feed you can give your animal, is that which is organically grown, but even organic plants may be mineral deficient. Your best protection is to add mineral supplements to your horse's diet.

→*"I own an eleven-year-old __Arabian mare__ who used to have a __club foot__. She was operated on and surgically fixed, but the foot still looked bad. I had trouble getting the blacksmiths to trim it properly, and when they did it wrong, it took ages for enough hoof to grow out to fix. When she tore the shoe off, most of the hoof wall came with it, and we really had a terrible time finding enough wall to nail to. She was a lazy horse and I had to push for everything I got from her when riding. She seemed to have little stamina and go crabby after a little work.*

*I put her on HOOF and RUSH CREEK 1:1 MINERALS and what a difference I have noticed in her. Her hooves are growing so fast the blacksmith can't believe it. When I told him what she was eating, he said "don't waste your money, those things don't work!" (meaning supplements for hoof growth). He can't explain why we are now trimming her every six to seven weeks and taking a good 3/4 of an inch off, when before we trimmed every nine to ten weeks and only managed to rasp a bit of hoof off. We never needed the nippers.*

*The side effects of the HOOF are a wonderful glossy coat, a strong healthy mane and tail and a mellow disposition. She just seems happy all the time, her ears are up and her eyes are bright and even after a tough lesson or a long show she seems to have lots of energy left."*
-Kathy Dorval,  B.C., Canada


• **ENZYMES**

As we mentioned in *ENZYMES in CHAPTER 1,* much animal food today, is processed. It is this heat extraction or cooking that destroys the digestive enzymes. Feed stuffs, such as soybean meal, plant protein by-products, molasses and others, are processed which kills the enzymes. Long term storage also can reduce the effectiveness of natural enzymes to process and deliver its food in the digestive tract. The horse, as do other mammals, produces its own antioxidant enzymes, necessary to fight free-radicals. Lack of minerals and lack of digestive enzymes will reduce their body's ability to create the antioxidant enzymes, leaving their immune system deficient.

→*"One day I came home late and my husband said that one of our **thoroughbreds**, Tiger, was suffering **intestinal distress**. He had suddenly stopped eating his hay and become very restless. He is a fabulous eater and to refuse to eat his alfalfa is a very BAD sign. I* *went and looked at him and saw that his face was pinched up, his nostrils wrinkled and his ears back, all signs that he was not feeling too happy. His belly looked rather bloated. I then remembered a friend who had a horse with a similar problem. I couldn't really remember whether she said she had used acidophilus and blue green algae or the enzymes and algae. While I stewed over this, it occurred to me that it didn't really matter. I'd feed both of them to him.*

*Ty loves anything with blue green algae in it. So I gave him a handful of enzymes and another handful of acidophilus. He grabbed a large mouthful and started chewing and then spit some of them out. I discovered it was the acidophilus he was rejecting. How animal know what they need, is beyond me! By now he had eaten quite a few enzymes and I thought, gee, this is going to get expensive. Just as fast, I figured if it worked, it would save an incredible amount of stress, not only on Tiger, but on all of us. Tiger was worth his weight in gold to us! Delaying treatment could have had disastrous results and expensive vet bills.*

*He ate about ninety enzymes as fast as we would given them to him. He then appeared to relax his pinched face and stood quietly for awhile. He then started to walk around and within ten minutes, lifted his tail and had a very large BM. He looked at us, ears up and face relaxed, and then strode off happily. Within a short time he was in the barn and begging for hay. We kept an eye on him for several hours, but he had no reoccurring symptoms. He ate his hay with great gusto, went out and grazed and was perfectly happy and content. End of problem."*

-Sharon Trump, Florida <small>Independant distributor.116796</small>

## • SUPPLEMENTATION

There are many tried and true folk remedies, handed down from generation to generation of breeders, trainers and farmers. Sophistication in supplementation has seen a dramatic drop in the pain and suffering of horses. We will include some of the newest and possibly less common known additional to oral and topical natural medications.

→*"I picked up a __standard bred two year old filly__, A.C. Faith, to break and train. It was the middle of winter and her coat was extremely long, so it wasn't until I caught her and was loading her onto the trailer, that I discovered her true condition. I was horrified to feel her ribs through her coat, and also found she had __barely any flesh or muscle at all__! Apparently, the owners didn't realize that the broodmares in the paddock with her were very aggressive and didn't allow her to eat. She was slowly __starving to death__.*

*When she got to my stable, I immediately fed her a warm bran mash with a little grain and lots of Timothy hay. The next morning, I noticed a smell coming from her stall that was really bad. I questioned several vets who assumed she needed worming and drugs. My nutritional doctor friend, Dan Promin, had encountered this situation before and explained that the odor was caused by the horse's system literally eating itself internally from lack of protein. The liver was near to shutting down and had to be toxic at this point. Had I given her the steroids as the vet's suggested, she would have died.*

*Dan immediately mixed up a powdered formula consisting of ground milk thistle seeds, that contains silymarin, an active ingredient necessary to detoxify and purify the liver. He added bromelain in a base of NUPRO Performance Plus for Horses which consists of kelp, bee pollen, biotin, yeast culture, flaxseed, MSM, DMG, alfalfa and lactobacillus acidophilus. Within two days, the terrible smell was gone from her manure. In a period of only one month, her flesh and muscle was returning to her body and daily exercising was making her stronger. She made a full recovery and was able to stand up to the rigors of daily training."*
-Janis Gianforte, New Jersey


•**Aloe vera**. Aloe has remarkable healing powers both internally and externally. It is a cleanser, detoxifier and normalizer. This plant contains anti-inflammatory agents and heals skin tissue, soothes and prevents scarring.

•**Biotin** is a B vitamin that improves metabolization of dietary protein and carbohydrates, and helps synthesize fatty acids. Feedstuffs differ widely in the amount of biotin they contain and a high proportion may be in a form that is unusable by the horse. Biotin is recommended by veterinarians and farriers to correct hoof and coat problems, to accelerate hoof growth, and as a dietary supplement for superior all-around health and vitality. Broken, cracked hooves, weak, thin hoof walls; inability to hold shoes; dry, flaky skin, dull coat; thin mane and tail are all symptoms of biotin deficiency. To be effective, biotin supplementation must be given daily over a considerable period of time. The therapeutic dose is 15 mg of biotin daily for an average size horse.

→*"Leo, and __eleven year old quarter horse__, was a favorite hack at a nearby stable. Al the riders loved him for his gentleness, his athletic ability and sweet temperament. For reasons beyond our comprehension, Leo was __abused__ and neglected, left in a straight stall with rotten, cracked and uneven boards. The manure was rarely cleaned out and he was not fed regularly, although he was worked every day. It wasn't too long before he was a __bag of bones,__ with huge, __festering saddle sores__ and __hooves that were severely crumbled and cracked.__ The vet believed he would not last more than a few more months, so we bought him because we could not bear to witness his deterioration.*

*A good feeding program, regular loving care and a lot of rest did wonders for Leo, but the most dramatic change in him was the quality of his hooves through daily use of GEN-A-HORSE, biotin supplement. In less than six weeks, his feet were no longer tender and he trotted and cantered willingly and with pleasure. His frogs, once so poorly defined that they were barely indistinguishable from the sole, were completely restored in three months. Another of our horses on this supplement, Sir Galahad, who displayed no hoof problems, is now better able to retain moisture in his hooves and needs much less hoof oil. After a month on GEN-A-HORSE, he grew a magnificent summer coat more beautiful and quite unlike any he had before. We now call him Sir Lustrous."*
-John Owens, New York

→*"In November 1985, my husband poured a concrete driveway, and instead of getting paid his fee of $750., he got a __race horse__*  *named Double Quack. The horse had earned $61,000 racing, but was put out to pasture with __chronic abscesses__, brittle, __cracked hooves__, __inability to hold shoes__ and soles with __soft spots__ the size of a quarter.* *Mr. Miller and I searched for a treatment and found GEN-A-HORSE, an equine biotin supplement created specifically for treatment of hoof ailments. After ten weeks, Double Quack was galloping again, his soft spots gone and he held his shoes full term. In five months, we took him to the race track and on August 16th, 1986 he won us $5000. A very nice profit for pouring a driveway."*
-La Johnna Miller, Louisiana

•**Blue green algae.** A nutritious source of amino acids, minerals, enzymes, vitamins and chlorophyll. It supports the immune system both in illness prevention and treatment.

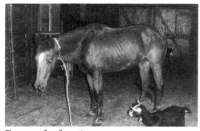
*Sunny (before )*

*Sunny (after)*

→*"The pathetic little __horse,__ named Sunny, caught my eye as I drove down the street. She was standing out in a large pasture, practically leaning on a tree to support herself and __heaving to get her breath__. Every rib in her body showed and she was desperately __skinny__. It was apparent from the way she was breathing, what her problem was. I had known the mare several years before when she grazed with my horses and she had been fat and sassy with a sleek coat. Now her coat was long and rough and looked as lifeless as she did. Her head hung down and she looked like she __wasn't going to last very long__.*

*I talked to the people boarding her and to the owner, and they confirmed my observations. The vet had been out and treated her, but the medication wasn't really helping. She wasn't eating much so her weight continued to drop. Her breathing was so labored it made me cringe to watch her. It took all her energy just to try and breathe, therefore she had none left over to be even interested in eating.*

*I agonized over her situation and finally insisted the owner put Sunny on Super Blue Green™ Algae. They agreed and so I added several capsules of Spectrabiotic (broad spectrum of friendly bacteria), plant based enzymes with the algae, co-enzyme Q10 and pet algae on her food. The owner and I both noticed a noticeable change in Sunny within fifteen minutes. When we turned our backs Sunny tried to eat her way into the canister of pet algae. Her body was telling her this was good stuff. I gave her more, and more sweet feed with more algae on it. She gobbled it all down.*

*Over the next few days she continued to improve. She was eating better and looking better and her breathing was noticeably better. Several weeks later, I stopped by to see her and she looked as bad as she had when we originally put her on the algae. The owner mentioned that she had run out and hadn't gotten around to getting more. She also hadn't been out to see Sunny. She just couldn't seem to confront the horse's illness and be there to take care of her. I called her and said I would take the horse and get her well and then get her a good home. I took her home just before Thanksgiving 1995 and by the middle of January 1996, she was well enough for a new family. She filled out, her breathing normalized and she looked like a completely different horse. She was enjoying the kids coming over to ride her and play with her. Her new family consisted of three young children who had never had a pet in their lives. They were thrilled to have a horse. Sunny reveled in the attention and was very gentle with them. Truly there had been a miraculous change in all of their lives."*

-Sharon Trump, Florida Independant Distributor 116884


•**Boswella** is a gummy extract of the Boswella Serratta tree commonly found in India. It has been shown to be useful against inflammatory diseases such as arthritis and chronic carpal joint dysfunction. It shrinks inflamed tissue by improving the blood supply to the affected area and enhancing the repair of local blood vessels damaged by the inflammation. It is good against stiffness and chronic pain from injuries such as stifle problems, sore backs, bowed tendons and bone spurs, soreness from hauling and hard footing. It is an alternative to Steroid use and growing in popularity with veterinarians, trainers and owners.

•**Carb loading Glycogen support with chromium.** Many horses do not utilize carbohydrates as well as others. When a horse ingests carbohydrates, they convert it into glucose. The pancreas then releases insulin to stabilize blood sugar levels and turn it into energy. The only problem is, every horse is different. Insulin resistance is commonplace in horses and it occurs when the insulin cell does not absorb the blood glucose, therefore not converting it to energy. This problem can be corrected by using a proper blend of carbohydrates and chromium to help the insulin mechanism work properly. This combination prevents the horse from Glycogen depletion and tying-up.

•**Chinese herbs.** Practitioners tailor the usage of these herbs to individual diagnosis of specific conditions for a specific animals. Over-the-counter herbs can be administered by individuals if they have an awareness of their animal's condition and consult a Chinese herbal practitioner or a holistic veterinarian using Chinese herbs. They assist healing by balancing the body as a whole.

→*"Mary Ann's __horse__, Jack suffered from __tumors__, or in Chinese medicine, an accumulation brought about usually by heat and stagnation. This horse was always gentle and easy to manage until the tumor began to increase in size. He then became irritable and badly behaved, intent on kicking anyone in his path. Mary Ann was a student at the Institute of Herbal Studies in Connecticut, and asked for a formula that would disperse the stagnation and invigorate the blood. She started using Survival (presently only available through vets), and after one week, the tumor showed signs of dissipating. The horse's temperament becomes once again, tame and gentle. The vet, upon checking out her horse, found that indeed the tumor had shrunk and requested the herbs be continued.*

*A diet of more cooling properties like mint and flowers helped to relieve the heat of the tumor and the quality of Jack's life was greatly improved. Although not a cure, Chinese herbs many times*

*can allow for a longer, healthier and happier animal on its path in this life."*
-Laura Mignosa, Connecticut


•**DMG.** Dimethylglycine (DMG) technically classified as a food, is found in very small amounts in some foods, for example, rice hulls. Chemically it resembles water soluble vitamins such as the B category. It removes lactic acid, helping to reduce muscle soreness and tie-up problems. It helps build the immune system, and increases oxygen supply to muscles for recovery from fatigue, giving more stamina and endurance.

•**Flower Remedies.** Each animal, and even humans can have underlying emotional issues that trigger disease. Since you may not get great results from taking your horse to the shrink, try flower remedies. Relieving emotional problems may be the key to the effectiveness of a remedy. For a complete listing read *FLOWER REMEDIES in CHAPTER 1.*

*Calming Essence or Rescue Remedy* are two very effective five-flower combination tinctures that effectively reduce stress.

*Crab Apple,* can help in eliminating parasites, open sores and the toxic condition of the horse's stressed body.

*Star of Bethlehem* can help with trauma associated with abuse or starvation.

*Sweet Chestnut* may help with depression and anxiety associated with extreme pain. These can be administered orally or through application topically.

*Black Walnut* is useful in times of change such as a move to a new farm or race track.. It has the ability to insulate the animal who feels vulnerable and unsafe due to readjustments. It will also help with hormonal cycles or seasonal adaptations.

•**Flaxseed** is an excellent source of essential fatty acids. Available in oil or as flax meal, adding this supplement to their feed will improve not only the condition of a horses' coat, but support their immune system as well.


→*"I have heard of several cases where **horses' hooves** that were severely **cracked**, healed completely in just a few weeks with only the addition of Fortified Flax to their regular feed."*
-David Nelson, Wisconsin

•**Garlic** can be the answer to curing many ailments. Clarissa McCord of Cloverdale, British Columbia tells of her use of aged garlic extract in liquid form to combat a virus that attacks horses. Characteristically, the disease passes from horse to horse and infects the entire stable. Ms. McCord owns the Cavendish Stables, and she is ever watchful for symptoms of the virus such as fever, coughing, mucus running from nostrils, fatigue, poor feeding and general disability.

Aged garlic extract was given to the young horses at Cavendish Stables, that had contracted the virus.

→ *"A bottle of liquid garlic administered on two successive days to each animal does the job of curing. One of my* **race horses** *developed the* **virus** *symptoms and was to be scratched from the racing program scheduled the following day. I gave one bottle of liquid garlic to the animal and he improved sufficiently to enter the race. He hit the board first, second and third."*

→ *"In another instance, 'Marty's Winter' and 'Candy Mistico' were given two bottles each of liquid aged garlic extract to control the virus that was running rampant in their bodies. They needed the remedy badly. They went on to race the next day and both finished in the money. A two year* **colt,** *named 'Victor' was in such* **poor shape** *he was not expected to develop into a race horse. After he took the liquid garlic over a brief period, he began feeling better and eating more. He has now qualified to take part in any races in which he is entered. As a stable owner, I have to admit that taking this aged garlic extract to the races pays off!"*
-Clarissa McCord, British Columbia

•**Glucosamine sulfate.** A natural compound produced in the body by the combination of glucose with glutamine, it acts as a building block for the skin, eyes, cartilage, bones and connective tissue. It is crucial to the strength and integrity of the joints and is an essential to creating hyaluronic acid which lubricates the joints. Studies have shown that glucosamine sulfate exerts an anti-inflammatory action, normalizes cartilage metabolism to help restore joint function and seems to have no known side effects. It is a wonderful alternative to cortisone for osteoarthritic conditions.

•**Green lipped mussel.** The official name is Perna canaliculus for this mussel from New Zealand. It is a rich source of animo acids, RNA, DNA, hyaluronic acid and glycoaminoglycans which promote the healing of soft tissues. Perna canaliculus has been shown to reduce pain and stiffness associated with arthritis.

•**Herbs (western).** Herbs work harmoniously in the body, encouraging healing naturally. Each plant remedy has well documented therapeutic uses and has been used by veterinarians since the 18th century. Most herbal remedies are used in minute dosages, well below concentrations that cause toxicity, resulting is few side effects. Stacy Small, editor with Karen Tappenden, of The Holistic Horse newsletter, recounts some case histories that caused her to develop herbal treatments.

→ ***On death's door.*** *"I was walking through Monmouth (NJ) Park Race track, when a trainer approached us with his vet, who needed help with a **filly** that they had just about given up on. Both men explained how they had tried seven different vet prescribed antibiotics on her. When I saw the filly,, she was a pathetic sight. She was depressed and depleted looking with thick mucus oozing from both nostrils and watery fluid running from her eyes. She didn't want to move because it forced her to struggle breathing.*

*"I discussed herbal treatments with the vet and trainer. We agreed we not only had to fight the infection, but also had to help build up her immune system which had been compromised by the large dosages of antibiotics. I suggested supplementing her with Vitamin C to support the lung tissue and was promptly advised that wasn't necessary because horses produce their own (unlike humans.) What did not make sense was how can a depleted animal be expected to produce the extra amounts of vitamin C that were required to help her. They conceded on the grounds that it could not hurt her. I gave her the Garl+C blend and in a few weeks, they called in disbelief. The thick discharge had cleared up. I explained that it was not my doing but the power of our friend the garlic, in conjunction with the vitamin C, and supporting her depleted state with adaptogenic Chinese herbs, that keyed specifically into the lungs. I don't think they heard the details since they were so thrilled to have her on the road to health. This depressed, droopy filly*

*showed signs of renewed life and was able to be put back into training."*

→***A bleeder.*** *"Boogie (a Grey Mare, 4 year old **Thoroughbred**), came out of a race that she ran poorly. Upon endoscopic exam, it was found that she bled badly and would need to be put on lasix (furosemide) for future races. The acupuncture vet told us that she bled worse from her right lung since that was the lung point that bled out during the treatment. He was barely able to get near her lung points to treat her because she was in such discomfort. He encouraged us to help support her healing process by developing a botanical blend that would tonify the lung tissue and attempt to restore elasticity to it, with a focus on the herbs that have a history of helping to prevent internal hemorrhaging. A product called "Bleeder's Blend" was created for her, and upon re-examination three weeks later, she showed signs of healing magnificently. At that time the vet could just about pound on her lung points without bothering her.*

*As a prophylactic measure, we were told by the attending vet, that we should use an Oriental Herbal blend as a pre-race, to help hold her from bleeding due to the stress of racing. "Yunnan Payaio" is a secret recipe that is kept closely guarded. It achieved acclaim during the Vietnamese War. Every soldier had a bottle in his "hit kit" in case he got shot or wounded. Not only can it be used internally, but externally as well to stop cuts from bleeding. We were encouraged by our vet to use this on all our bleeders, not as a replacement for lasix, but as an additional stop gap measure. We did find that it allowed us to reduce the amount of lasix, which was great since lasix it is a strong diuretic and depletes the body of potassium."*

→***Major surgery avoided.*** *"Turner (a Brown **Mare**, 7 years old Thoroughbred), was retired from racing as a six year old. We decided to breed her since her pedigree and race record was very impressive. During her first foaling, the colt came through and **tore her vaginal** cavity into the rectum and the colt had to be pushed back in order to be delivered properly. The vet told us she had a large tear (4-5" long) and would need surgery to repair it. It was explained that she would need to be sent to a clinic since she would*

115

*have to be anesthetized and put on a table for major surgery. We were also warned that she would be prone to infections and most likely miss the next breeding season. We discussed helping her with an herbal blend and reviewed the goals we needed to achieve. We were told we needed to not only needed to combat infections and to promote healing, but help to restore tonicity to the uterus and nourish her system to rebound from the depleted state her body was now in. The vet wished us luck and said he would be back in a few weeks to check her and get her ready for her trip to the hospital. We were determined to avoid the trauma of shipping her and the newborn foal to the clinic and the separation that was pending.*

*The "Broodmare Blend" was the result of this research. We selected a variety of herbs that had a long history of use as uterine tonics with all the nourishment a new mom needs, since she has to feed her offspring. We also put her on Garli+C Blend to help combat the predisposition to infection. Upon re-examination a few weeks later and prior to surgery, the vet was in awe at how fast the mare healed. The tear was down to the size of an eraser head. Turner was able to have it sewn up in a simple procedure done right in her stall with the foal by her side. We were told there were no signs of infection and she could most likely go to the breeding shed thirty days after the surgery. We beat the odds by helping her body to heal on its own and spared her and her foal, the physical and emotional trauma of surgery and all its side effects."*

→*Mares and PMS? "In reality, they seem to suffer from the same symptoms that females of all species have to deal with. Many years ago, I was doing equine therapy work at the track and on farms. Owners, trainers and vets were calling me in to work on these mares that were perfect in conformation, had no history of injuries and were basically uncomfortable and needed attitude adjustment. The therapy work seemed to give them short term relief, but didn't get to the root cause. One day I asked myself, "Why can't mares go through PMS?"*

*Most of the vets I had been working with were men who couldn't possibly understand what PMS is like and how it feels. They laughed when I suggested this notion. Since there were no animal formulas for this syndrome, I was forced to look at the standard formulations for people. I tried a few before settling on the "Tang Kuei 18".*

116

*Here was a blend that seemed to take away the tightness and crampiness in the ovary area, and greatly changing their attitude. Malicious, cantankerous animals that did not want to be touched, reverted back to the happy free moving animals they once used to be. Seeing is believing. Now, many of the vets that had laughed at me are sending the clients to us for the "Tang Kuei."*

→ **Horses with sniffles**. *"Upon a visit to one farm, I noticed that all the weanlings had runny noses. They looked so pathetic standing there rubbing their faces on the buddies, painting them with yellow and green goo. I asked the farm manager what they do about this and the answer was just to let it run its course. It's all part of growing up. I found this response difficult to swallow. If it was a human child you would find a mother frantically looking for a cure. Why shouldn't young horses be given the same chance for relief. They agreed to let me try herbs on them. We added powdered Echinacea to their feed and lo and behold the yearlings began clearing up in a matter of days. The other foals in other pastures were still running around with crusty faces. Each year, come spring, I get a phone call from the farm manager, placing an order for Echinacea."*

•**Herbs for foaling.**   Raspberry leaves mixed in with grain will strengthen uterine walls and is helpful for gestation, labor, delivery and post-partum repair. Blue cohosh and squaw vine are also beneficial for the uterus. Goldenseal facilitates healing and soothing of the uterine and vaginal membranes after foaling. It can assist with post-partum hemorrhage. Redness and edema of the vulva can be helped by applications of calendula (marigold). Calming Essence or Rescue Remedy, both flower essences, can assist in calming the animal down during the stress of delivery.

•**Hesperidin.**   An important bioflavionoid ingredient, hesperidin strengthens capillaries. This helps prevent pulmonary hemorrhaging during stressful performance. It also builds immune response to disease and aids the respiratory system for breathing.

•**MSM.**   Methylsulfonylmethane (MSM) is a nutrient sulphur metabolite of DMSO. It helps joint and muscle flexibility, relieves arthritic and inflammation conditions and gives connective joint

117

support. This important sulphur nutrient is lacking in many horse's daily diets.

•**Oxygen Enhancers** are useful, especially for animals who exert themselves, such as racing dogs or horses. Adding oxygen supplements to your pet's diet helps enhance nutrient absorption and can be a powerful respiratory aid.

•**Probiotics.** These "friendly" intestinal bacteria digest food, and make vitamins and minerals available to the body. The pH in the intestines varies from acidic to neutral and is regulated by minerals. The small intestine, where digestion occurs, is home to Lactobicillus bacteria which facilitate this process. The large intestine acts as a storage tank for absorption of toxins, and when pathogenic bacteria find shelter here, they are prevented from creating illness due to the immune system and digestive fluids. If the pH is disturbed through improper diet (as happens in a sugar rich environment) or from ingestion of antibiotics, the unhealthy bacteria travel from the large intestine to replace the "friendly" bacteria, Digestion is now compromised and nutrients are not absorbed properly. Many different types of illness can appear, most likely camflouging the cause as bacterial imbalance.

To keep the "good" guys in control, we must be conscious of applications that upset the digestive balance. As we mentioned, antibiotics reduce the numbers of the "friendly" bacteria. So do dewormers, over-vaccination, dietary changes and even stress and psychological upsets. The best protection for the digestive system is balancing your horses diet and using nutrition to keep their immune system strong. Supplementing with Lactobacillus and Bifidus bacteria will help the body produce vitamins and crowd out the bad germs by overwhelming the with shear numbers. Young foals that have a problem with chronic diarrhea, have been treated using probiotics, rather than antibiotics (which further upset the natural culture in the digestive tract.) Yogurt is used by some veterinarians because the active cultures it contains help the digestive system. Enzyme supplements can also assist in this task. *Caution*: Probiotics should be administered when the pH is in balance (consult a practitioner), so they will have the opportunity to multiply. If the pH is out of balance they will die and you will have just wasted money on the supplement.

If you are transporting your horse over long distances, you may add probiotics to his diet. In critical situations, these fermentation assistance products have meant the difference between a horse making a smooth transition to his new location, rather than experiencing him being off feed, losing weight and possibly coming down with colic symptoms. Once at the new location, probiotic cultures should be continued to get his fermentation back in action. Light exercise can also help your horse stimulate intestinal mixing and passage of gas that may have built up during the trip.

→*"Shadow, my dearest friend, is a thirty-four year old __retired hunter/jumper__. Three years ago I came close to ending his remarkable life. At thirty-one, he was showing the effects of accumulated years of hard work in the hunt field and show circuit. When he developed some __inexplicable swelling__, __stilted movement__ and a __lethargic attitude__, the vet administered treatment to the horse and advice to me. He said his treatment might not help Shadow and it may be getting time to put him down. I was advised not to wait too long.*

*The anti-inflammatory medication for the horse took effect. The advice to me did not. Instead, I added A.B.C's PLUS to his diet. That was three years ago and nowadays the vet is amazed. He is strong, alert, moves well, and most of all seems happy to be living his life, playing with his pasture friends and watching his human friends lovingly dote on him. He is a joy to see and a wonder to behold!:"*
-Gigi Hoelscher, Alabama

•**Seaweed.** Seaweeds are the most fascinating plants in the world. They are an extraordinary "treasure chest" supplying both nutrients that are beneficial for many health problems. As they grow, they are constantly nourished by the ocean waters which contain every element that the body could need. The mature plants are composed of more than sixty minerals and trace elements (naturally chelated by the plant), and a broad array of vitamins, amino acids, antioxidants, essential fatty acids and phytochemicals. Many other complex natural compounds in the seaweeds are undergoing keen scientific investigation for their antiviral, antitumor and immune potential properties. Seaweeds also contain compounds which enable the body to bind and harmlessly excrete certain toxic heavy metals.

At a time when foods are becoming more deficient (due to ingredient processing and years of soil depletion from farming practices), our animals' metabolic systems are being asked to work harder. Not only do seaweeds provide nutritional tools to help overcome dietary deficiencies, they also provide natural compounds with therapeutic health benefits. Many people think that kelp and seaweed are the same thing, however, only four of one hundred sixty-four different botanical families of seaweeds are kelps. Seaweeds provide a rich natural source of iodine, but there can be too much of even a good thing. Horse owners should use caution if feeding kelp meal (particularly from Laminaria kelps), because it may contain levels of iodine high enough to create goiter problems, especially in pregnant mares.

Seaweeds are harvested from the water, dried and then ground into meal. The nutritional quality is affected by the harvesting and drying methods. Since not all seaweed products are the same, request information from the manufacturer as to purity and content. High quality seaweed meals will make an extremely beneficial addition to your animal's diet.

→*"I'm convinced that if it weren't for the nutrients in seaweeds, my big-hearted three-day event horse, Hull, would never have had the chance to fulfill his potential and become Reserve **Horse** of the Year in the United States. For years, he had suffered from **poor hoof condition**, in spite of the finest care and feeds available. An imported seaweed product helped, but I was frustrated by the inconsistent quality from batch to batch. This led to developing better processing methods and blending different seaweeds. Friends and fellow competitors who had seen the improvements in Hull began asking for some of my "stuff", and the product known as SOURCE was born.*

*Over the years, we've received thousands of letters from owners whose animals have been dramatically helped by the nutrients in seaweeds. Unfortunately, when you talk about all the different kinds of good results, it starts to sound like "snake oil". It's not surprising though, when you realize that micronutrients affect virtually every physiologic process in the body, and they're all available in the seaweeds."*
-Susan Domizi, Connecticut

•**Spirulina and Chlorella.** Spirulina is a planktonic blue-green algae that is high in protein an vitamin B-12 and is different from most algae in that it is easily digested. Scientific studies show that spirulina strengthens the immune system, causes regression and inhibition of cancers as well as inhibiting viral replication, which renders the virus harmless by the body's defense system, thereby eliminating it. Spirulina is also high in GLA essential fatty acid, making skin and coat shiny and soft. It feeds the beneficial intestinal flora and is excellent in alleviating symptoms of arthritis. Spirulina is also good at treating parasitic or bacterial infections. Chlorella is a cultivated algae that is a good sources of protein and chlorophyll. It is useful to enhance immune systems and to fight infections. Veterinarians have found that wound healing, blood counts and performance improves in working horses given these wholesome algae..

•**Tea Tree Oil.** The most potent source of this antiseptic and antifungal substance is extracted by steam distilling from the foliage of the melaleuca alternifolia from New South Wales. Some varieties are labeled organic, some are not. Tea Tree Oil penetrates the skin and mucous membranes and can promote tissue and cell growth, healing a wound. It is useful on skin disorders, saddle sores, cuts, fungal infections in hooves.

•**Vitamins.** Supplementation of feed with vitamins may be prudent. A few are discussed in this section. Vitamin D is a necessary ingredient of any horse's diet. It can become deficient, especially in winter, if horses are kept inside, away from sunlight (*see section on LIGHT in CHAPTER 1*). Supplementation of vitamin D can be found in sun cured hay. Vitamin E, an antioxidant, is also essential for increasing breeding performance. It is also one of the most important vitamins for the prevention of muscle tie-ups and soreness. Supplementation will increase endurance and stamina along with improving fertility rate and resistance to disease. Vitamin B (Thiamine, riboflavin, niacin, choline, pantothenic acid and B12) are needed and are added to many processed feeds. Vitamin A, (from carotene), an antioxidant, is found in leafy green hay and carrots, a favorite of horses. This vitamin is stored by the horse and used during winter months when "veggies" are scarce.

Normally a horse's liver produces water soluble vitamins (B & C), if it is functioning properly. Unfortunately, compromises in feed have produced unhealthy digestive systems, thereby restricting the production of these essential vitamins. Horses may no longer manufacture sufficient quantities of ascorbic acid (vitamin C) to counter the effects of aging, stress, breed predilections, environmental afflictions and poor quality feed. Owners of horses that were in pain and unable to be ridden, saw an improvement in soundness when calcium ascorbate mineral supplements were administered. Vitamin C has been shown to play a role in a number of biochemical reactions in the metabolism of collagen, in the immune system and as an antioxidant. Vitamin C, is rapidly excreted from the body, sometimes prior to its utilization. A more bioavailable form of this vitamin, calcium ascorbate, provides rapid absorption into the cells of the body.

Traditional therapy for degenerative joint disorders in horses have only a low success rate, with many horses becoming progressively worse despite treatment. Formal clinical trials using Ester-C calcium ascorbate, were made on horses with particularly severe degenerative joint diseases and lameness. Over the course of the trials, all of the subjects were taken off any other therapy. Of ten horses observed, nine of them showed good to excellent response to Ester-C. The study concluded that this treatment gave symptomatic relief of degenerative joint disorders, allowing a good percentage to return to functional status as riding horses. Ester-C calcium ascorbate supplements have also been used in horses with chronic pulmonary obstructive disease (CPOD), or heaves.

→"One year ago, I was considering putting down, my **horse** Cheyenne. She was suffering and was **unable to eat, lie down, exercise and stop coughing**. I was giving her several medications just to help her comfort level, but as time passed, the assortment of medicines had either a temporary effect or none at all. I then tried C-Flex (Ester-C). One year later, I find myself treating Cheyenne just like the other horses and almost forgetting that she even has any illness. Cheyenne's life has substantially improved as a result. She now is able to share the barn with the other horses and stay inside during severe weather. In the past, she would have to stay out of the stalls due to the indoor dust and her constant coughing.

Cheyenne now is ridden on a regular basis and can keep up with the other trail horses without rest "breathing" stops. She now eats her grain rations and her hay or grass. She no longer "parks"

*herself stretched out in the corner of her field with her meal only half eaten. Cheyenne is medication free! Cheyenne is cough free! Our son has literally been given his horse back. Shaun says, "Cheyenne is fine now and she'll be around for years." I think with C-Flex, this just may be true!"*
.-Jan "Jay" Yount, Winchester, VA


→*" The first time I saw Gus, I could not even tell what color __horse__ he was. He was caked with dirt and sweat. After a bath, I discovered he was a bay, but very dull and unkempt. His ribs were showing and his hips stuck out where the muscle had wasted away and his neck was thin and scrawny. He was __on his way to the slaughter house__ and definitely looked the part. His eyes were dull and showed no feelings. Gus was also lame.*

*I took Gus home and helped him recover. The reason for my horse's lameness was because he suffered from __arthritis__. We decided to try a new experimental product, Ester-C, that our vet recommended. We did Flex Training on Gus to see how bad his arthritis was. After we had flexed his knee, we jogged him out and he fell flat on his face. The Ester-C helped Gus improve immediately. He became sound as the months progressed. Even the X-rays of his left fore knee and his right hind ankle showed improvement. Now Gus is 100% sound and the only thing remaining in his arthritic joints is scar tissue. He continues on the Ester-C, morning and night. Gus' sweet disposition and his willingness to learn has made him a champion. Thanks to the Ester-C , arthritis is no longer stopping Gus from performing in three-day eventing and he is pain-free and supple."*
-Jessica Miller, Virginia


Sometimes vitamins may be ineffective as absorption will not take place if the digestive system is not functioning properly. Therefore, work on balancing their diet, possibly adding enzymes, essential fatty acids and probiotics so vitamins will be assimilated.


→*"With all the variable feed stuffs we had to use on our Kennebunkport, Maine to San Diego, California cross country trip, our __horses__ maintained a consistent appetite and performance while using A.B.C. PLUS. Once because of logistics, we were without this*

123

*supplement for two weeks and saw a dramatic change in the performance of the horses. The decision was made at that time, not to be without A.B.C. PLUS and we still include it in our daily feeding program."*
-David Helmuth, Trainer/Driver numerous North American hitch's including Country's Reminisce Hitch

•**Yucca** is useful as a laxative, diuretic and antiseptic. It is helpful for ulcers, sore joints and arthritis and as a pain reliever and also an effective anti-viral and anti-fungal agent.

• **WATER**

As outlined in *WATER in CHAPTER 1,* living beings will die if they don't get water. Animal bodies consist of between seventy to seventy-eight percent water: five percent in the blood plasma, fifteen percent in the fluid between the cells and fifty percent in the fluid within the cells. If animals get poor quality water, they may get sick, and unless it has been identified as a waterborne pathogen, you may not know that water was the culprit. Proper amounts of water are necessary to help a horse regulate body temperature, digest their food, act as a solvent for many chemicals ingested, aid respiration and keep the liver and kidneys functioning. Water should always be available for a horse. With each pound of feed, your horse should drink three pounds of good quality water.

Many times horses are given water that people would never drink. Many times horses are given city water full of chlorine, fluoride, etceteras, etceteras. Chlorine disrupts cellular metabolism causing weight gain, potential cancer and many other illness'. If it is impractical to give your horse bottled water, at least install a filtration unit on the supply line. These can filter out sediment, chlorine, fluoride, heavy metals and many other toxins.

If you horse drinks polluted water, you may want to detoxify them. Fasting cleanses are absolutely not recommended, rather choose either homeopathic preparations, blue green algae, chlorella, spirulina, minerals, garlic, or other herbal remedies. A healthy horse's immune system can probably tackle most bad "things" that appear in water. If the chemical assault from water sources is prolonged, cumulative effects could start taking their toll on the animal's health. At least one manufacturers has created a supplement that has the ability to protect livestock and horses from herbicides, insecticides, pesticides, nitrates and pollution found in drinking water. Even with this "helper", toxins can accumulate over time creating long term illness, therefore you must consider giving your horse the same clean water that you drink.

Many livestock producers tend to under estimate the value of water as an essential nutrient. In many cases, laboratory reports indicate a level of a specific substance and yet no explanation is given as to the meaning of these values. The following is information on standard levels of some of the various compounds found in water.

•**Nitrates** can affect the oxygen-carrying capacity of hemoglobin. In animal nutrition, nitrates in the water can also interfere with normal digestion, gestation, growth and health. When hogs are exposed to water high in nitrates, they will probably scour, appear to have vitamin or protein deficiencies and may exhibit arthritic symptoms. Normal growth and health are visibly impaired. Nitrate compounds interfere with the proper digestion of the animals even though the feeding program is adequate.

•**Nitrites** are dangerous in water supplies, although concentrations occur at low levels. Nitrites are considerably more dangerous than nitrates because they can cross the intestinal wall rapidly, get into the blood stream and combine with hemoglobin which makes it impossible for the hemoglobin to carry oxygen.

•**Sulfates** are found in almost all natural water supplies due to the solvent action of water as it filters through the earth. High sulfate concentrations can cause sever digestive disorders. In farm livestock, this can mean a continual scouring problem that cannot be eliminated by antibiotic supplements.

•**Salts** can affect the intake of water and thus performance. Animals can eventually become conditioned to the salinity if it is not excessive.

•**Bacteria** if found in water, means that some sort of pollution is occurring. Cases have been reported in which contaminated water served to infect animals when the animals were maintained for an extended time on the contaminated water. Bacteria should be filtered out for maximum health.

•**Iron** in two forms, ferric and ferrous, can cause digestive disturbances and scours if high levels are found in water. This is particularly prevalent in young animals. It makes feed nutrition not available by tying them up so they cannot be absorbed.
-*information above provided by Advanced Biological Concepts*

## EPILOGUE
Every horse owner has their own regime for feeding and unless the horse gets ill, they may not care to look at alternatives. We hope we have opened your mind to some different ideas (or at least reinforced the ones you already have.) Education is a wonderful avenue, and by being introduced to new treatments and products, your animal may continue in good health further into the future. Holistic approaches to health can prevent sickness and fortify the immune system. We don't expect you to try all the measures outlined in this chapter, but please, do further research. The resource directory at the end of this book, lists companies that specialize in keeping your animal healthy. Contact them for more information. Your horses will be happy you are finally discovering what they knew all the time!

-for more information on alternative treatment for horses, request THE HOLISTIC HORSE newsletter: 115 15th St., Surf City, NJ 08008 (609)-494-4215

# CHAPTER 5. NATURAL NUTRITION FOR BIRDS

## Alicia McWatters, M.S.

*This chapter is dedicated to all bird lovers who are interested in the satisfaction and rewards of providing a natural diet for their birds.*

*Budgies*

We are most certainly in the beginning of a natural diet renaissance and many aviculturists are developing an awareness of nutritious foods as preventive medicine and, as a result, learning about how to create better health for their birds. While there are a number of diets and bird products in the marketplace, my goal is to educate bird owners toward a natural way of feeding their birds. I feel very strongly that the best diet in the world for our birds is a home-made diet consisting of fresh foods and appropriate supplements. It is quite simple to do correctly and efficiently, and the health rewards are both great and obvious.

Offering a large variety of foods is as important to our bird's health, as it is for ourselves. Primarily herbivorous, in the wild, birds instinctively look for the proper plants, flowers, seeds, nuts, berries, and other foods to nourish and heal themselves. These foods would contain helpful and curing substances, *not* synthetic copies of what the plant used to be. In a captive environment, it is our responsibility to provide them with similar foods, which contain the complex nutrients required for a healthy bird. The foods we serve should closely resemble the forms in which they are found in nature (unrefined, unprocessed, with no added chemicals, and organic if at all possible).

Most veterinarians who practice holistic medicine agree that our birds should not be fed a fabricated, commercial bird food. Processed, denatured feed often creates disease while, whole natural food offers life, energy, and optimum health. Many of these commercial diets contain chemical additives which are potentially harmful to our birds' health, as outlined in *FOOD in CHAPTER 2,*. All life is missing from these diets due to the refining, processing techniques. Nutrition-oriented veterinarians, often suggest fresh foods made at home from scratch. These veterinarians use nutrition as a key tool in the treatment of illness and in the prevention of disease. When we talk about preventive medicine, ultimately we are talking about nutrition. The best way to provide a balanced diet when feeding fresh food is by offering our birds a wide variety of foods, with moderation as a guide.

The basic nutritional content of this chapter applies to all avian species. While the majority of parrots thrive on a vegetarian-type diet, there are other birds, such as certain finch species and soft-billed birds, such as toucans and mynahs who require live foods (i.e. insects, larvae and small vertebrates) along with fruits, greens, and some seeds. Some live foods can be home-grown or commercially purchased, such as meal worms, white worms, ant pupae, fruit flies, fly larvae, aphids or crickets.

Certain parrots, such as those from the Loridae family, require nectar pollen and a variety of fruits to thrive, but they will also eat small quantities of plant food and seeds. Most birds relish germinated seeds as an additional bonus to the diet. I will later in this chapter, touch on the preparation methods for properly sprouting seeds. Environmental health is also an important part of keeping our birds in top condition, and so I have concluded this chapter with ways to enhance this aspect of their health while also including environmental and physical safety guidelines.

"Your immune system is your interface with the environment. If it is healthy and doing its job right, you can interact with germs and not get infections, with allergens and not have allergic reactions, and with carcinogens and not get cancer. A healthy immune system is the cornerstone of good general health."        -Andrew Weil

## • IMMUNE SYSTEM BASICS

Our health is only as good as the strength of our immune system. This means that we heavily rely on our immune system's 24 hour a day service in order to remain disease-free and healthy. Under normal circumstances, our immune system does not cease its attempt to keep us symptom-free. However, as many of us know, some of our birds do fall ill from time to time, while others do not. When illness occurs it simply means that your bird's immune system is not functioning at its optimum capacity.

There are many reasons for a less than optimally functioning immune system. Dietary and environmental factors play an important role in the relative strength or weakness of our bird's immune system. By enhancing the diet and reducing the toxic substances in their foods and in their environment (water and air) we can greatly strengthen their immune system. Genetics appear to also be a significant factor in the susceptibility to disease; however, if a hereditary weakness is discovered, a healthy diet and environment can often reduce or relieve many of the symptoms, while enhancing and lengthening life.

In general, researchers and scientists have long been aware that inadequate nutrition causes a depressed immunity and the susceptibility to a host of pathogens. Malnutrition has been associated with a wide range of illnesses, from rickets in growing youngsters to various bacterial, fungal, and viral infections.

Foods high in vitamin C, beta carotene (a precursor to vitamin A) and E, plus the mineral selenium, work as **antioxidants.** These help free the body of the daily toxins (known in the body, as "free radicals"), which come from our air, water, some foods, radiation, toxic metals, stress, and other harmful environmental conditions. Antioxidants act as scavengers, devouring the free radical particles and protecting our bird's health.

Foods which have a beneficial effect on the immune system are those in the cabbage family, (i.e. kale, broccoli..), and many other fresh organic vegetables, fruits, and grains. Other natural nutrients known to boost the immune system are trace minerals, zinc, calcium, bioflavonoids, chlorophyll, found in green vegetables, algae, the amino acid argenine, and the vitamin B complex. Fish oil supplements are also stimulating to the immune system. Herbs which are beneficial to the immune system are echinacea, goldenseal, astragalus, and garlic.

ANTI-STRESS NUTRIENT.

N,N-Dimethylglycine (DMG) is a amino acid, nutritional supplement which helps to alleviate stress during illness or injury. It has been used successfully as the following report indicates:

→ *One of the negative aberrations of __wildlife rehabilitation__, and in particular with certain species of birds, is their low tolerance to*

*captive stress, As a rehabilitator of raptors and songbirds, I am always looking for ways to decrease the <u>stress</u> of handling these birds. I discovered the benefits of a natural anti-stress nutrient known as N,N-Dimethylglycine or DMG. It helps to oxygenate the birds cells, acts as a detoxifier and stimulates their immune system. I have observed birds who, under certain conditions, would have typically shown symptoms associated with captive stress (<u>rapid breathing, increased loss of muscle mass around the breast bone, lethargy, lack of self feeding, death,</u> etc.) recover better than expected. Some birds survival rate increased and some were released back into the wild sooner. I administered Vetri-Science Vetri-Liquid®DMG in their gavage or with hydrated food. Songbirds are given the DMG by dropper either alone or with their oral antibiotics.*
-Jean Semprebon, Certified Wildlife Rehabilitator, Vermont

A bird owner's further success with DMG is reported by David Hertha, DVM in Huntsville, Alabama:

→*For roughly a month following a bout of liver problems, an <u>African Grey Parrot</u>, who had an extended vocabulary, showed a tendency towards <u>one phrase over and over again</u>. This raised concern by the owners (and a slight annoyance). The bird was treated with a daily dose of a naturally occurring immune stimulant, Vetri-Liquid®DMG. The veterinarian explained that his experience in treating birds with stress related behavioral disorders or immune related diseases had been very positive. After several weeks, the bird's vocabulary returned to normal.*

## • NUTRIENT REQUIREMENTS

Birds have a high metabolic rate, for instance, parrots require a diet rich in complex carbohydrates, such as whole grains, legumes, fruits and vegetables with their abundance of vitamins and minerals. Foods, which contain a high-water-content, such as raw fruits and vegetables are ideal for they are easily digested, provide our birds with enzymes, and other life-promoting elements. Raw foods are what our birds are biologically adapted to, therefore the best results will be obtained by offering them. When selecting food for your birds, choose wholesome fresh, unrefined, organic foods and I believe, seventy percent of the food they eat should be water-rich foods.

There are no universally accepted requirements for specific nutrients for birds. Although all birds require the same nutrients, each bird is biochemically and genetically unique. Therefore, their quantitative nutritional needs will differ. Each species (or individual) may require more or less of a particular nutrient; such as one may require a higher or lower level of fat, protein, carbohydrate, vitamin, mineral, or water in the diet, and their caloric needs may vary. The amounts of nutrients required by an individual bird is also influenced by its age, species, size, sex, environment, activity level, hormonal status, stress, illness/injury, nutritional status and the type of diet consumed (its bioavailability). Lifestyles of our birds should be a deciding factor in the quantities of what we feed, and changes made when appropriate for the various stages they encounter throughout their lives (i.e. growth, molting, and breeding).

Each nutrient has its own specific function, but no nutrient acts independent of another. All of these nutrients must be present in the diet in varying quantities. Food processing/refining and soil nutrient depletion all play a part in vitamin/mineral deficiencies which result in symptoms and the illnesses associated with them. It should be remembered that while one bird may metabolize a nutrient sufficiently, another may not. We then have to determine why (such as a digestive disturbance), which can sometimes be helped by an enzyme supplement, probiotics, or a correction in diet. Often just by adding a higher level of the particular nutrient(s) in question, we find that an improvement in health begins to take place.

## NUTRITION SCIENCE IS NOT AN EXACT SCIENCE.

Nutrition science, being the result of estimation, is rarely exact or completely accurate. When manufacturer's claim that their diet is exact, I am quite leery, as one can only get within a ballpark range of accuracy. Also, each bird is an individual with varying needs. This must be kept in mind when creating a diet. A fresh diet will provide a much broader range of nutrients in a whole complex form, whereas most commercial feeds are synthetically produced and offer its nutrients in isolation of one another. It is also far easier to overdose on a nutrient when it is offered in a synthetic form.

When thinking about the nutrients in any diet we should understand that some nutrients are stored in the body for later use, such as the fat-soluble vitamins A, D, E, and K and the essential amino acids. So it is not necessary that your bird receive every known nutrient every single day. As long as your bird is eating a balanced varied diet each day (not too much of one thing) you can rest assured your pet will be receiving what it needs.

"People think that if they simply take vitamins and minerals they will be healthy, but every vitamin and mineral requires an enzyme. You can eat pounds and pounds of vitamins and minerals, but if you don't have the proper enzymes they won't work."    -Lita Lee, Ph.D.

• **ENZYMES**

Enzymes in our bird's diet are also vitally important and they can be obtained in fresh, uncooked foods or through supplementation. Food enzymes assist in proper digestion of carbohydrates, fats, and proteins and are gradually destroyed at high temperatures. This means that cooking our bird's food or feeding those foods which are commercially available, which utilizes excessive heat, are also void of enzymes. There are many types of enzymes at work in our bird's body at all times. Enzymes perform may tasks, such as maintaining health and proper metabolic function of the body, strengthening the immune system, and aiding in the digestion of food. They are substances which make life possible. Enzymes work synergistically with vitamins and minerals. Vitamins/minerals cannot do their job of keeping the body healthy without the presence of enzymes, as enzymes and vitamins/minerals are dependent on one another for all the necessary biochemical activities of the body. Foods which have been chemically-treated with pesticides or grown in nutrient-depleted soils may also contain a low enzyme content.

The dry convenient diets (pellets) have been denatured, then the essential synthetic nutrients are added back. They are devoid of enzymes which are life promoting elements. While they may maintain life, they do not promote optimum health or longevity! Food enzymes are very sensitive and are easily destroyed by low moist heat (105-118 degrees F) or dry heat around 150 degrees F. While a bird's digestive organs produce some enzymes endogenously, internal enzymes and the beneficial intestinal bacteria can be damaged

132

by chlorine in drinking water, certain medicines, air pollution and chemical additives. If the foods we serve are low or deficient in enzymes, the digestive organs must work double time to produce more enzymes. Eventually the body become less efficient in doing so and the body begins to draw enzymes from other parts of the body, such as the blood, organs and the immune system. Food (plant) enzymes facilitate optimum health, therefore, fresh raw foods should form a large part of their diet. Whenever cooked foods are fed, you can sprinkle a plant enzyme supplement over these foods to assist the digestion process. Fresh vegetables, fruits, and sprouts contain an abundance of these energy-giving enzymes and when offered regularly may inhibit illness and disease.

## MALABSORPTION.

Malabsorption of nutrients is a serious problem and its symptoms can include: weight loss, dry skin, feather loss, weakness, fatigue, and anemia. Those birds which suffer from this syndrome generally require more nutrients than others. An enzyme or probiotic supplement, along with an improvement in diet may be helpful in improving the absorption of nutrients. In some cases, certain nutrients may need to be offered in a more easily assimilated form, in older birds. These would include powders, liquids, or on occasion, an injectable form, as advised by your avian veterinarian. Additional causes of the malfunction of absorption can be stress, certain medications, over consumption of processed foods, refined sugars/carbohydrates, an enzyme-free diet, an imbalance of the intestinal bacterial flora (candida), intestinal parasites, diarrhea and/or constipation, diseases of the pancreas, liver, and in turn result in digestive disorders. Under normal conditions, absorption is dependent on the body's needs; a bird who is deficient in a vitamin/mineral will absorb more of it than one who is sufficiently nourished.

## • ORGANIC FOODS

The foods we ultimately choose to feed our birds, and this includes our outdoor wild birds, is a very personal choice. This decision is based on what we have been taught by our veterinarians, breeders, other bird owners and the media through advertising. Some of this information may be valid, while other times, sadly, it is not. By educating ourselves, reading labels, and understanding that the feed we choose can have either a positive or negative effect on our birds, we can more readily provide them with the best diet possible. Choose to feed organically grown produce whenever possible. Organic produce not only generally tastes better than conventionally grown, but is higher in vitamins and minerals. On the other hand, conventional produce, grown in nutrient depleted soils, has been shown to have a lower vitamin/mineral content. Subsequently, they have less value to offer the consumers of those foods. Wild birds fed pesticide laden seed, have faced reproductive disorders and behavioral changes.

Over 2.5 billion pounds of pesticides are dumped on crop lands, forests, lawns, and fields annually. There can be anywhere from four to 25 different pesticides used on conventionally grown produce. Tolerances are set for only individual pesticides, without consideration of the combined health effect of multiple pesticides in the conventionally grown foods we consume. Additionally, most individual pesticides have not been fully tested for their health implications. Many scientists are concerned about the long-term health effects of these chemicals, and feel that they may be responsible for the rise in immune deficiency disorders, nervous system, reproductive and hormonal problems, many cancers and other life-threatening diseases. The toxic pesticides, chemical fertilizers, growth stimulating chemicals which are used to rapidly, abundantly, and flawlessly grow fruits and vegetables may be potentially harmful to our bird's health.

The organic farmer's primary goal is "prevention". Organic farmers use natural methods of eliminating pests, such as insect predators, traps, barriers, mating disruption or may use botanical or other non-toxic pesticides if needed. These farmers are committed to growing their crops in nutrient-rich well balanced soils, whose benefits are then passed on to us and our birds. While organic products may cost a bit more, we feel they are well worth the extra cost. However, with the growing awareness of the value of organically grown produce we should soon find a decrease in the price as more and more people are purchasing these foods for themselves and their pets. If you are unable to buy organic produce, spray them with apple cider vinegar or 3% hydrogen peroxide, to remove external pesticide residue, wait 5 minutes and rinse; particularly on apples and greens. Organic agriculture can provide our family and our pets with the best nutrition, while also keeping our environment clean.

## • DIET FOR CAGED AND WILD BIRDS

One of the biggest concerns voiced from bird owners is their inability to encourage their birds to eat a variety of fresh foods; hence, assure that their birds are consuming the necessary nutrients. Since this has not been a problem for me, at least not on any long-term basis, I'd like to share how I prepare, store, and serve a fresh food diet to our parrot flock.

Preparing a fresh diet consisting of wholesome ingredients need not require a drastic adjustment in preparation. In fact, with the "mash" diet, preparation is done in advance at your convenience. This method of feeding, eliminates the daily slicing and dicing of fruits and vegetables. We make up ten days worth for nearly twenty pairs; which takes about one and a half hours to complete. Then, serving is as simple as scooping out the correct amount for each bird or pair. You can modify this recipe for feeding only one bird.

To begin, all ingredients are put through the food processor *briefly* (with the exception of certain foods eaten readily), and then scooped into a large pot (stainless steel preferred) for mixing. Note: Remember to always place a cover over the pot in between adding an ingredient to prevent oxidation. The mash is then placed in air tight containers and stored in the freezer. Remove and place in refrigerator for thawing, well in advance (30 to 36 hours for a five cup container).

Scheduled feeding times are at 8:00 am (mash) and 2:00 p.m. (seed mixture), simulating the natural eating patterns of birds in the wild. The 8:00 am feeding provides them with enough to fill their crops throughout the morning hours. Although each pair is treated individually, about 1/2 cup per pair is the average (for medium-sized parrots). Adjust properly for a single bird. As you learn how much each bird or pair will eat in each time period the amount can be adjusted so that none is wasted. Any uneaten mash should be discarded after four to six hours to prevent spoilage, which, if eaten, could cause a bacterial infection. Special care should be taken in this

135

matter, particularly in the warmer months. These frequent feeding times will also allow you the opportunity to observe your birds often, which is very important in keeping you closely in tune to their overall health. Feeding times may vary and are adjusted to your schedule.

## MASH INGREDIENTS FOR PARROTS.

*Frozen organic vegetables* - (corn, green beans, carrots, peas) 12 lb.

*Fresh organic vegetables* - 1 lb. parsley, 5 large tomatoes, 3 chayote (fed raw), 3 medium sweet potatoes or yams, 4 medium white potatoes (fed lightly steamed, skins included).

*Bean mix* - (1/2 cup each of the following beans and peas) black-eyed peas, pinto beans, kidney beans, adzuki beans, green and yellow split peas, garbanzo beans, black beans, soy beans, mung beans. (Rinse and drain well, soak in cold water 6 to 8 hours in refrigerator. After soaking they are boiled for 10 minutes, simmer for 20 minutes, using only enough water so that none is left after cooking, to preserve valuable vitamins).

*Grains* - (1/2 cup each, added to beans, soak, and boil) wheat berry, pearl barley, triticale, brown rice

*Organic greens* - (fresh grown) comfrey and/or mustard greens. Comfrey, (an herb) which provides vitamin A, B-complex, C, & E; one of the few plants known to contain vitamin B-12, normally found only in animal protein foods. Up to 33% protein is contained in the leaves and it is high in minerals. Mustard greens (about 1 dozen large leaves are used), are high in vitamins A, B, C, calcium and iron (frilly-leafed and broad leafed are available).

*Organic Fruit* - 5 large bananas, 5 large apples, 1 1/2 lbs. of grapes fed whole, (1/4 cup strawberries or cranberries seasonally)

*Seeds* - (1/4 cup each) pumpkin seeds and sesame seeds, both provide calcium along with zinc, which aids in fertility. Sesame seeds also provide an additional source of 8 "essential" amino acids which cannot be manufactured by a parrot's body.

*Vitamin and mineral supplements* - 1/4 cup powered kelp (contains iodine, therefore helps to prevent thyroid disorders, such as goiter), 1/4 cup Blue Green Algae or Alfalfa powder (aids in digestion, strengthens immune system, contains essential fatty acids, and is nutrient dense), sprinkle of Kyolic® (garlic), Apple Cider Vinegar and Calcium Magnesium Liquid.

The recipe above can be used as a guide for a healthy diet. You may

substitute an item for another equivalent food; for instance, if a particular one is seasonally unavailable. Collard or dandelion greens in place of comfrey or zucchini in place of chayote are examples.

*Tiffany eating mash*

## SEEDS ARE A NUTRITIONAL PART OF A BIRD'S DIET!

Contrary to what you may have been told about seeds, they are a very good source of nutrients! Seeds and nuts eaten raw or sprouted contain many of the vitamins, minerals, essential fatty acids, and amino acids essential for the growth and maintenance of healthy skin and feathers. Sprouting increases the nutrient value, especially the vitamin content. Seeds contain the best natural source of essential unsaturated fatty acids that convert nutrients into energy. We offer our birds seeds not only for the pleasure they receive from eating them, but as a boost to the immune system from the many important nutrients they contain! Seeds are rich in vitamin A, E and the B-complex vitamins, and if sprouted enzymes and vitamin C. These natural antioxidants are extremely valuable to your bird's health by helping to prevent illness and disease. The minerals they contain are calcium, magnesium, manganese, iron, zinc, copper, molybdenum, selenium, chromium, silicon, potassium, and phosphorus. Sesame seeds, sunflower seeds, and almonds are excellent sources of calcium!

Without a doubt, seeds are a very important part of the diet! Our seed mix, which is offered as the evening meal, makes up about 30% of our birds' diet. Some of the seeds we serve are: millet, sunflower, sesame, almonds, pumpkin, flaxseed, and buckwheat. Of course, be sure your seeds come from a quality source. We purchase a variety of seeds, mostly organically grown, from a health food market. Seeds must be stored carefully to prevent rancidity caused by oxidation of their fat content. Do not buy too far in advance and store them in tightly cover containers in a dark, dry, cool location. Particularly vulnerable are sunflower seeds and peanuts. The majority of our birds' diet consists of fresh organic fruits, vegetables, grains and legumes, and seeds are an especially valuable part of this diet for their super nutritional qualities!

Since birding is America's fastest growing outdoor hobby, we should follow these nutritional guidelines with outdoor wild birds. The National Wildlife Federation® worked together with Natural World Interactions to produce a high quality birdseed for wild birds. Since most people won't mix and fortify their seed, they can now purchase packaged natural bird seeds, which are fortified with vitamins, minerals, amino acids, enzymes and antioxidants. These natural seed mixes don't contain artificial flavors, colors, preservatives and bulk fillers such as milo, wheat, oats, buckwheat or rice. Most birds find all of these fillers undesirable and will push or throw them on the ground converting your "bargain" bird food to expensive squirrel food.. Now our backyard feathered friends can enjoy the same healthy food as our indoor pets.

If we avoid preservatives and additives in *our* diets, why shouldn't we consider doing so for our wild friends who depend on us for their winter survival. The seed they choose in the summer doesn't come with additives, therefore their bodies may not be prepared for this artificial assault. Giving them a natural seed mix is like giving them a vitamin pill, and they will appreciate it by telling their friends to come to your feeder. A word of caution, don't stop feeding wild birds when the weather starts to get warm. Many plants are not producing seed until the summer, and since birds begin nesting in the spring, they will need to make trips to your feeder.

→ *"My husband and I no longer have young children or grandchildren running about, so we decided to get a bird feeder for our backyard. We spoke to friends who fed __wild birds__, and they said the two biggest problems they had were the bigger birds that bullied the little birds and __keeping squirrels out of the feeder__. We went to a presentation about feeding wild birds and afterwards bought a Wings EcoFeeder, designed to solve the bird and squirrel problem. To our surprise, this feeder actually did keep the big birds away. They would try to land, but lost their balance. The squirrels can't find a comfortable resting place on the feeder either, so are content to remain on the ground and wait for scraps to be tossed over.*

*We bought some Wings Super-Seed DeLite and a few other brands. We were interested in seeing which **birdseed** attracted more birds. When the Wings was used, there was less seed waste on the ground and there was so much chirping going on, you'd have thought we were feeding the entire bird population on Long Island. I guess birds aren't any different than humans; they know **what they like**. We are requesting information from the National Wildlife Federation on their Backyard Wildlife Habitat Program. We are truly enjoying our new hobby and look forward to many years of watching "our birds" and their families. "*

-Gail Scherer, New York

SPROUTING SEEDS, GRAINS, AND BEANS.

Sprouted seeds, grains, and legumes can enhance your bird's diet by adding a nutritious supply of vitamins, minerals, enzymes, chlorophyll, and high-quality protein. Each seed contains all the nutrients necessary to sustain life, but remain dormant until they are placed in the right environment to begin germinating. When air, water, and a suitable temperature are provided, the seeds begin to sprout. It is at this time that their energy is released and all of the essential nutrients are made available. As the sprouting process continues, carbohydrates are converted by the biocatalytic action of enzymes into simple sugars. Complex proteins are converted into simple amino acids and fats are transformed into fatty acids, which are easily digestible compounds.

Sprouts are an excellent source of A, B, and E vitamins, calcium, potassium, magnesium, iron and important trace minerals; selenium and zinc. When sprouted, nature miraculously increases the total vitamin content and creates the addition of vitamin C in each little shoot. Sprouts can be offered to your birds at the time of harvest, losing none of its nutritional value. Sprouts and other raw foods are natural sources of antioxidants, preventing environmental pollutants from damaging our birds' bodies.

As beans are an incomplete protein, combining any dried legume with one or more grain ensures a complete protein meal; supplying up to 25% amino acids. Certain legumes contain complete protein: lentils, soybeans, and peanuts. Many seeds, such as almond, pumpkin, sesame, sunflower and buckwheat, are complete proteins. However, most seeds and beans served alone would contain an inadequate balance of the essential amino acids. As a result of combining and serving our birds various seeds, or beans and grains, we are increasing the quality and value of the protein in their diet. Variety is the key!

Beans and other seeds contain enzyme-inhibitors in their dry form. The process of germination neutralizes these inhibitors, releases the enzymes, and places these foods in a more bioavailable form. Enzymes are made up of protein and are responsible for all your bird's bodily processes. For example, enzymes maintain proper function of their body by regenerating cells and tissues; keeping their vital organs healthy. They stimulate the production of antibodies which fight infection, while they also aid in the digestion and metabolism of food. Enzymes, are an essential part of our bird's diet and they are found in foods which are in their natural unprocessed form, such has fresh fruits, vegetables, and raw sprouted seeds. Cooking and processing destroys enzymes between 105-118 degrees F, as well as a large percentage of the vitamins in foods. Minerals in cooked foods are no longer chelated, and therefore are more difficult for your bird's body to utilize. These foods slow down the rate of metabolism and weaken the immune system leaving open the chance for illness and disease. When foods are eaten raw they are a good source of food enzymes that aid in the digestion of starch, protein, fat and cellulose. These substances can then be absorbed by the body for optimum utilization. "Live" foods help to conserve the body's enzymes, stimulating metabolism and the regeneration process, contributing to long and healthy lives.

For success with home sprouting, use quality seed, avoiding seeds and beans which are chipped, pale or not evenly colored. Be sure they are certified edible (organic preferred!) and have not been chemically treated or dyed. Some of the beans and seeds easily sprouted are sunflower, sesame, mung, lentils, alfalfa, chick peas, buckwheat, pinto, adzuki, and kidney. There are many ways to sprout. Containers can include jars, colanders, strainers, trays, baskets and special bags. No matter which method you use, the procedure for growing is the same. Soak seeds in filtered water overnight, then in the morning, pour off the water and place them in your grower. Rinse twice a day with clean water. Different seeds sprout at different times, but most are ready in three or four days. Further details on sprouting can be found in the book, Sprout It! by Steve Meyerowitz, published by the Sprout House.

To take it one step further, you may also plant a variety of seeds and offer fresh grown greens to your birds. Not only are they healthier than store bought, they are also a breeding stimulant. The gathering of greens from our garden is routinely done and our birds seem to thrive on them. Some of the greens we grow are safflower, canary, millet sprays, wheat, plus many medicinal herbs, such as garlic chives, comfrey, chicory, lemon balm, dandelion, valerian, echinacea, peppermint, and chamomile. These are used for a variety of health purposes in either a fresh, dried, or liquid form. They may be offered as preventive medicine or for illness for their beneficial qualities. Of course, knowledge of the properties of herbs and their correct application must be acquired before their use.

You may grow some of these plants indoors, in flats, plastic, or clay pots, either from seed or established herbage from your local nursery. These plants can be brought to an outdoor garden area in the spring or they may remain indoors. Place in a sunny location where they will receive a minimum of six hours of sunlight or broad spectrum artificial lighting. For best results always use a rich, quality soil, keep well drained, and fertilize weekly. If insects become a problem, spray with soapy water or use natural pest repellent sprays to eliminate them. Remember to thoroughly rinse your greens before serving.

If your bird(s) only seems to enjoy dry seeds, such as is typical of many Australian species; sprouting their seeds can be the answer toward providing them with all the vital nutrients for a healthier, more active pet. Birds, which were raised on an all dry seed diet naturally are stubborn to try anything new, as they normally fear the unknown or anything they do not recognize. To overcome this, you can first try offering their seeds soaked (for 24 hours). After they've accepted these, then offer them in the sprouted form, and finally as seedling grasses. Moist seeds can be fed in the morning and the dry seeds (in smaller amounts each day), in the evening. Then, gradually introduce the sprouts or seedlings. Once these are accepted as something edible or at least tolerable, eventually introduce other fresh foods, such as vegetables or a slice of apple, orange, etc. The process of offering the seeds in various stages should progress slowly, but surely. How quickly results occur will depend on the age of the bird and how long he/she has been receiving a dry seed only diet. Eventually, your patience and persistence will payoff and you will have a happier, livelier bird.

If time is short and you just can't sprout, use high quality substitutes like wheat grass, alfalfa, barley grass, or algae (super blue-green, spirulina, chlorella) powders. Sprouting, and growing your own greens will provide your birds with a healthy treat for all seasons. Your birds will receive up to 100% nutrition as a result of the miraculous sprouting process! We use sprouts and greens more abundantly during breeding times and they are given as part of the weaning diet. At other times, they are given more sparingly, up to three times a week. It is easy, inexpensive, and your birds will thank-you for it!

## • SUPPLEMENTS

Kyolic® Aged Garlic Extract™ can be sprinkled over the mash daily for its benefits in aiding digestion, stimulating the immune system, and keeping your birds resistant to infection and disease. Gloria Dodd, DVM mentions that "veterinarians have been successful at treating birds with liquid aged garlic extract for Candidiasis and related illness (1 1/2 teaspoons should be mixed in their water daily until symptoms are gone)." We use Apple Cider Vinegar (ACV) over the mash using a plastic squirt bottle. We use 1/2 tsp. for medium to large-size parrots, 1/4 tsp. for smaller species. ACV is an immunity enhancer; it's natural antibiotic action protects your birds from infections. It is rich in enzymes, potassium and other important minerals, while also aiding in digestion and the assimilation of food. An organic non-distilled brand is recommended. Oxygen Enhancers are useful, especially for caged birds who live in an indoor environment which may not be as oxygen rich as outside air. Adding oxygen supplements to your bird's diet helps enhance nutrient absorption and can be a powerful respiratory aid.

The high phosphorus ratio versus calcium in most foods requires an increase in calcium through a quality supplement. The ratio of calcium to phosphorus, should be 2.5:1, including D3. Extra calcium is provided daily by the use of Calcium Magnesium Liquid for the requirements of the African Greys, while other species receive it regularly with frequency depending upon age, activity level and breeding cycles. Juvenile birds (under 1 year) and pairs which are aging or less active receive it more often, as are birds prior to and during egg laying, and while raising young. Remember that birds under stress (which includes extreme heat or cold) need additional calcium, as well as an increase in all essential nutrients. We add 1 tsp. of the Calcium Magnesium Liquid daily to the mash for each pair of

Greys; other medium-sized birds, e.g., Amazons and Pionus use 1/2 tsp. per pair. Small birds, such as cockatiel size, use 1/4 tsp. per pair. Large parrots, same as for Greys. Reduce amount for a single bird.

This seed mixture, is meant to complement the mash diet nutritionally, It is served in the afternoon, and makes up about 30% of their diet. All seeds are useful and beneficial, but you must be sure they come from a quality source. Ideally, some can be grown in your own environment, if space permits. The basis of our raw organic seed mixture is hulled millet 80%, hulled sunflower 5%, shelled peanuts 5%, rolled oats 5%, and buckwheat 5%. The most important nutritive elements of seeds are the B-complex vitamins, vitamins A and E, unsaturated fatty acids, protein, phosphorous, and calcium. For example, pumpkin seeds, sesame seeds, and sunflower seeds are high in protein, plus all of the above vitamins as well as magnesium, zinc, iodine, and potassium. The value of seeds, nuts, and grains along with beans and peas, are unsurpassed, especially in the sprouted form. Sprouting seeds will increase their total vitamin content and may be added to the morning mash. Seeds also have a positive effect on birds by supplying quick energy, beak stimulation, and are certainly healthful in rationed amounts. Over indulgence of seed, especially fatty seed (such as sunflower, peanut, etc.) may crowd out other essential foods from the diet and can therefore result in nutritional deficiency as well as obesity. Your seed mix should be stored in a cool, dry place, away from direct light, and in air-tight containers to prevent rancidity caused by oxidation. Some protection from rancidity will be provided by vitamin E which is a natural anti-oxidant, and present in varying amounts in oil-bearing foods. No more than six weeks worth should be purchased in advance.

Vitamin A deficiency is common in birds. Symptoms may include allergies, sinus trouble, sneezing, susceptibility to infection, rough dry skin, as well as abnormal hormone activity, possibly creating reproduction problems. Vitamin A aids in the growth and repair of body tissues and helps maintain smooth disease-free skin. Internally it helps protect the mucous membranes of the mouth, throat, lungs, and gastrointestinal tract, thereby reducing the chance of infection. To ensure prevention of this deficiency we supplement their diet with vitamin A, D, and Omega-3 fatty acids from cod liver oil. A natural source of vitamin E is provided by wheat germ oil. While vitamin E assists in greater storage of vitamin A, it has also been shown in many studies to increase fertility and reproduction, and may improve stamina. You can mix 1 tbs. per lb. of seed mix, or 2 to 3 drops (per bird) in their soft food or seed mix, slightly less for small species and a bit more for larger species.

We have had excellent results with this mash method of feeding our birds, and it is enjoyed by all. Initially, as with any new thing it may take a short period of adjustment to become accustomed to it. Birds will readily adapt to this new diet if given gradually with their old diet until they are receiving the mash only. Generally speaking, for most of our flock it was a matter of a few days, with the exception of a few stubborn ones, that took a little longer. With new birds it is always helpful to have a good avian role model nearby, one which can show these birds to accept the mash, as birds learn quickly by observing others.

In the wild, about two thousand species of birds regularly ingest pollen from flowers. They sense that pollen is a densely packed source of high quality nutrients in a primal level of the food chain. Caged birds do not have the luxury of hunting for pollen. Honeybees have done their work for them by packing these microscopic grains into a single large granule which can be fed to your pet. In a 1972 study (Salajan), when feed rations included bee pollen, egg laying increased seventeen percent in the first sixty days, the yolks were richer in color and there was improvement in gonadotropin levels at the histological level. Birds of all species can benefit from the inclusion of this source of rich, natural and superior quality nutrient supplement.

Providing our birds with a natural foods diet may take some time and effort, but the results are well worth it! Of course, as hard as we try, we cannot duplicate the diet they would receive in the wild. If more research in aviculture and nutrition is acquired, (with their captive lifestyles in mind) we may gain more knowledge. However, foods fed in the "live" (mostly raw) form certainly are superior and come the closest we can get to a natural diet. This is essential for your birds' physical, mental and emotional health. It will increase their resistance to infection and disease, by strengthening their immune system. It surely represents the basis of preventive medicine. Our job is to make their lives, as nearly as possible, long, active, and productive.

If a commercial diet must be used I recommend one made without synthetic preservatives and additives, though an enzyme supplement is suggested to promote efficient digestion. Most importantly, a quality commercial brand is preferable to a homemade diet done incorrectly. If you are not going to take the time to prepare a fresh diet *right*, then please don't do it at all.

• **ENVIRONMENTAL HEALTH**

The veterinarian who is environmentally conscious will ask the question: What are the underlying dietary and environmental causes of, and contributing factors to, my patient's symptoms?

CLEAN WATER.

Water is a vital element to life. The body's water supply is responsible for and involved in nearly every body process including digestion, absorption, excretion and circulation. Water is also the primary transporter of nutrients throughout the body. Water helps maintain a proper body temperature and for carrying wastes material out of the body.

Clean water is imperative to your bird's health and we highly recommend a water filter for your home. There are many different types of water filter units on the market which are affordable. Choose one which has had a high rating for eliminating bacteria, Giardia, chemical wastes, chlorine, fluoride, lead, and many other common water contaminants.

An electrolyte fluid which is "sugar-free" is a necessary additive to most water supplies. Sugar feeds unwanted yeast and bacteria, therefore its use should be limited. This solution may be used in small diluted amounts for hydrating new chicks by providing the following minerals: potassium, magnesium, calcium, manganese, and chromium, so essential for a healthy chick's body. These minerals also help to alleviate the stress which is often a common symptom in birds experiencing temperature extremes, during breeding times, and any time when there is change in their environment, diet, or social relationships. It is essential to provide trace minerals supplementation in any drinking water, because most household water sources have been treated and the minerals filtered out.

## CLEAN AIR.

Another healthy item to have in your bird room is an air purifier or filtration unit. A HEPA (High Efficiency Particulate Arresting) air cleaner is used to cut down on bird dander and house dust. These are particularly helpful if a family member has allergies. Some of these units may also help to eliminate bacteria, viruses, and other airborne particles. Ozone air purifiers that come equipped with a negative/positive ion charge have been found to be extremely effective. They not only reducing mold, airborne pathogens and chemical fumes from decorating materials, but because of their ionizer, aviaries have seen a calming effect and behavioral changes whereby birds pick at their feathers less.

## HUMIDITY.

It is often wondered, "W*hat is* the ideal humidity for birds?" This is a difficult question to answer as each species comes from a different climate and altitude. At our home in the Sandia Mountains., 7000 feet above sea level, the humidity is generally on the low side with the average between 20-30 %. At monsoon season, however, the humidity rises to 100% at night, slightly less during the daytime. For our desert climate, 30-40% would be considered a comfortable level. Some of the South American Pionus species which we keep and raise are originally from a similar altitude to ours here in the mountains of New Mexico.

Some Australian species, e.g. certain species of cockatoo, cockatiels and budgies are from a semi-arid climate and may be comfortable with a lower humidity level. Conversely, those species which come from the lowland, rainforest and tropical zones may appreciate a higher humidity level.

Sometimes a species may be distributed over a widespread range of territory, some parts drier and other parts containing more moisture. Since each species comes from a different atmospheric condition, altitude, or their region may overlap, we can best meet their needs by knowing about the geographical area which they originate.

Birds are remarkably adaptable when healthy and strong. We feel very fortunate that our birds acclimated so easily to our environment here in the mountains versus our former home near the ocean in southern. California. However, we feel nutrition and appropriate supplements have made a major contribution to their adaptation to our drier climate. Some of us own a variety of birds with each one from a different climate. In this case, a middle range of 40-60% may best suit the needs of the various species we keep.

You can increase the humidity level in your bird's environment by placing a humidifier in the bird room. Many bird owner's use a warm mist humidifier during the winter months when household heating systems create a drier environment. If you place a hygrometer in the location of your bird's cage, you can monitor the percentage of humidity in their environment. Be sure to disinfect the humidifier thoroughly between water refills.

LIGHTING.

If your bird is kept indoors and does not receive any direct sunlight, we recommend full spectrum lighting. These lights come in florescent bulbs or tubes that attempt to simulate the full spectrum of natural sunlight. We use the tubes, in 4' shop light fixtures (purchased from a hardware store), that are hung from the ceiling. For convenience, we have ours on an automatic timer, which is scheduled to turn on shortly after sunrise and turn off shortly before sundown. We consider this lighting system to be as vital to our bird's life as clean air and water, and nutritious food. Lack of sunlight can adversely affect your bird's behavior, endocrine system, central nervous system, muscular system, skeletal system, immune system, and inhibit disease prevention.

Just like humans, they can develop the SAD (seasonal affective disorder) syndrome from lack of full spectrum light wave lengths. Dr. John Ott, developer of the Ott Light links natural sunlight and health. He says, " My studies have indicated that light is a nutrient, similar to all the other nutrients we take in through food, and that we need the full spectrum range of natural daylight.." One breeder of exotic birds found that by installing radiation-shielded full-spectrum fixtures, his flock became calmer and his Emus were laying earlier and with stronger eggs. Birds have been helped in many ways by this type of lighting as the following story depicts.

→"Our organization, Volunteers for wildlife, have treated over 500 **birds**, 200 mammals and 22 turtles in 1995. We started using Lumichrome full-spectrum lighting for prevention of **metabolic bone**

147

*disease in young passcrine birds and they have been useful to mockingbirds, robins and endangered plover species as a source of UVB irradiation, so crucial for avians and helps in the auto-manufacturing of 1.25 dihydrocholecalciferol. The Lumichrome IXX fluorescent lights really brought out the various pigments in the center's box turtles' scutes only after a few weeks of UVB supplementation. An increase in overall vitality and feeding response was easily observed. This was especially crucial for those turtle's which needed to be kept active during the fall and winter because of injuries and general health. I'm so impressed with these bulbs that I've used them on my green iguana and monitor lizards at home. Already I've seen more orange-yellow pigmentation develop in my male iguana, even out of breeding season. Although nothing beats time under the sun, the Lumichrome bulbs seem to be about as close as one can get!"*

-Samuel M. Lee, Volunteers for Wildlife, Huntington, NY

*Notes on feather picking-*

Most birds take pride in their feathers and keep them in good working condition. Under normal circumstances where our birds are healthy and are provided with the elements necessary to meet their needs, much care and effort is devoted to their daily grooming routine with feathering picking not a part of this practice. Something is seriously amiss physically, psychologically, and/or emotionally if you notice your bird suddenly missing feathers or deliberately damaging them. If excessive, long-term feather picking occurs it may cause follicular damage, such as folliculitis, and the absence of feather regrowth. A balding bird has lost some of its thermo-regulatory abilities and is probably undergoing some stress. If your bird seems to be perpetually feather picked either by itself or by its overly affectionate mate, bear in mind that their quantitative nutrient needs increase. At these times they would require higher levels of proteins, fats, carbohydrates, vitamins and minerals, similar to that which is needed during the normal molting period.

Skin and feather disorders are often manifestations of an unhealthy environment or poor nutrition, which result in a depressed immune system. Some other reasons might be: inadequate rest, sunlight, fresh air, humidity, or exercise. Also, cold, dry winter weather or hot, dry summer weather can be damaging to our bird's skin and feathers. Other common causes include stress, boredom, infection (i.e. fungal, bacterial, viral, or parasitic), genetics, chemicals, certain medications, a diet consisting of excess refined foods and sugar, poor digestion and assimilation, ailments such as liver malfunction or a hormonal dysfunction, (i.e. hypothyroidism), essential fatty acid depletion, iron or zinc deficiency, or food allergies. The list goes on. A nervous bird who preens excessively may eventually develop skin tumors. These are generally limited to the upper back, dorsal wing, and in the uropygial area (preen gland). Your avian vet can exam your bird and carry out the appropriate lab work to try to determine an accurate prognosis. If physical disease is ruled out, a behaviorist or nutritionist may be very helpful, because stress factors or malnutrition are frequently the underlying cause of feather-picking.

Using an air purifier to reduce airborne pathogens can have a beneficial effect of reducing feather picking. Some of the nutrients known to be useful for skin/feather-related disorders are vitamin A, E, the B complex, zinc, and the essential fatty acids. These can be found in a numbers of natural foods or by offering a quality nutritional supplement. We use flax seed oil for it is rich in linoleic acid, linolenic acid (essential fatty acids), vitamin A (beta carotene source), E and promotes healthy feathers, skin, bones, and nails. We recommend 1 tbspn. per lb. of seed mix. This supplement must be kept refrigerated.

SKIN THERAPY.

We use the following hydrating herbal therapy to replenish dry skin: Calendula: aids in the healing of dry, cracked skin; Chamomile: soothes and softens skin, reduces inflammation and swelling, helps aid healing; Elder: softens skin. Whenever dry skin becomes a problem for my birds I make up an "herbal mist". This can be made quite simply by preparing one or more of the above herbs and placing the warm solution in a mister bottle. Recipe: 4 cups of boiling water/3 tsp. of fresh herb leaves/flowers/bark (placed in a stainless steel or porcelain infusion ball). Let steep for about 10-15 minutes in measuring cup then filter tea through a cheesecloth or strainer into mister bottle and it's ready! Or you can purchase a ready made herbal electrolyte spray mentioned in the Resource Directory. Spray your birds thoroughly and don't forget their feet where they may need it the most!

## DANGERS INSIDE AND OUTSIDE THE HOME.

Remember a home with a pet bird must be 'birdie-proofed' just as though you have a toddler in the house. The only difference is the bird will possess toddler inquisitiveness all of its life! So please be cautious about the following items to avoid tragedy.

**1)** _NEVER_ allow your bird freedom while someone is cooking or ironing. Ironing board covers contain toxic Teflon™ Be sure to be careful not to let a Teflon™ pot or pan cook dry or burn. It will emit toxins which could KILL your bird!!! If using Teflon™ (polytetrafluoroethylene) pots or pans for cooking, please, be sure to use them properly and never walk away from the kitchen! No, not even to answer the phone! There have been too many tragic stories of bird owners forgetting about the dinner cooking on the stove while using Teflon™ cookware. If the pan burns it will emit toxic fumes and the subsequent result will be the loss of your birds. It is so very easy to do. So if you are inclined to forget, do not use Teflon™!!!

_Do not_ use household aerosol sprays or chemical pesticides in or around your home. These products can harm your bird's delicate respiratory system, causing lung damage, or worse, death. Instead, use safe, natural alternatives. Keep your bird safe from all types of cleaning agents, i.e. detergents, soaps, etc. and other toxic substances, such as painting supplies and any other agents which emit toxic fumes. Also, please _do not_ smoke in your bird's environment. Fresh, clean air is paramount for the health of your bird.

**2)** _DO NOT_ take your bird near a pool, bath tub, or other body of water, to prevent the drowning of your bird. Keep the toilet bowl closed.

**3)**Check your bird's wing feather growth at least every 2-3 months. _Do Not_ neglect this important bird owner's responsibility. **Q.** How do you recognize when clipping is needed? **A.** Once blood (purple in color) in feather shafts have receded into the follicles, full growth has now taken place. It is now safe to clip your bird's wings at this point. We suggest the ten outer primary feathers be clipped on each wing. Clipping is done facing the top of the bird's wing; be sure you do not clip the secondaries. Both wings are clipped equally. In between clipping, you still need to be careful near windows, open doors, ceiling fans, mirrors, etc. Supplies needed for wing and toenail clipping are large scissors, nail clippers and flour or corn starch for bleeding. You should also have on hand an emery board for filing and smoothing toe nails.

If a blood feather is damaged and bleeding remove it by pulling it firmly from the base of the quill with a pair of needle-nosed pliers. Hold pressure on the follicle until all bleeding stops. In a case where bleeding occurs from a broken blood feather and you do not have pliers handy you can spray the site of injury with cold water from a mister bottle. Or you can apply an ice-filled compress and pressure to the site of injury.

4) *NEVER* leave your bird unattended at any time!!! Keep your bird caged when he/she is alone. *Do Not* leave your bird in an environment freely with other animals, (i.e. cats, dogs, etc.) No matter how calm and good-natured your other pets may be, you can not trust nor predict an animal's motives ahead of time. Enjoy your pets separately and with undivided attention.

5) *NEVER* leave your bird in a vehicle in hot weather for any length of time. Even a short period of heat exposure may cause heat stroke or hyperthermia and death. Misting with cool water and gradually bringing down the bird's body temperature to normal is helpful should this incidence occur.

6) We don't recommend you bring your bird outside (unless securely caged) as even a bird whose wings are clipped may fly away out of sight if startled by a vehicle, loud sound, child, etc., or if a strong wind occurs.

7) Keep your bird away from electrical wires, fireplaces, and woodstoves. Keep them safe from cookware, furniture and household items which contain toxic metals, such as aluminum, lead, copper... Also, cages which contain lead, zinc (galvanize), or where lead-based paint has been used, such as on wrought iron, are all harmful. Metal poisoning can cause anemia, symptoms of mental depression, confusion, loss of memory and many other disorders. An advanced case of metal toxicity could lead to death. *Note*: White vinegar may be used to neutralize zinc on galvanized wire by spraying it on the cage during the first cleaning. Rinse thoroughly after waiting a period of 30 minutes.

151

**8)** Food bowls should be stainless steel, or glass such as corning ware. Do not use utensils or bowls which have been enameled or glazed. Cadmium a toxic metallic element is often used to achieve the colors in enamel. Many ceramic glazed bowls contain lead and so should be avoided. *Note*: A lead test kit can be obtained from most hardware stores and some bird stores. Be sure to change food and water daily. Fresh food should be removed after four to six hours to prevent bacterial/fungal growth. Use filtered or purified, uncontaminated water.

**9)** New carpeting can emit chemical vapors which may be toxic for your bird or yourself and can be the cause of allergic reactions and/or respiratory distress. Consider natural alternatives such as cotton, wool, sisal or jute. Be sure any new synthetic carpeting is aired for at least two weeks prior to its installment. Always keep windows open for an entire season after installing synthetic carpet and purchase an air purifier to oxidize the chemical fumes. There are hundreds of toxic chemicals in synthetic carpet and no one really knows what happens to the body when they are mixed together.

**10)** Formaldehyde, found in carpets, permanent press and stain resistant fabrics is also used as a preservative in wood and in glues used in common particleboard furniture. It is potentially dangerous and toxic if the materials containing it are chewed and ingested by your bird. Avoid using materials containing this chemical for any of your bird's needs, such as for building nest boxes, wall dividers between cages/aviaries, household furniture made with veneer or particle board, and the glue used to hold the furniture together may also contain formaldehyde.

**11)** Be sure to identify all plants in your bird's environment and remove all potentially toxic plants which they might come in contact with.

### • SYMPTOMS OF ILLNESS

If your bird is exhibiting any of the following signs or symptoms of illness, contact your avian veterinarian:

•A decrease in energy level and alertness (stress, nutritional deficiencies, infection, allergies, adrenal, thyroid or liver disorder),
•Sudden decrease in appetite (stress, infection, hypothyroidism, GIT

disorder, parasites, however, appetite can fluctuate somewhat and be quite normal)

•Dull, droopy eyes (they should be normally bright and clear, no discharge or redness)

•Nasal discharge (sinusitis, rhinitis, allergies, a dry environment),

•Chronic sneezing (bacterial or viral infection, allergies, a dry environment)

•Bad breath, white plaques in throat, or canker sores in mouth (fungal infection or vitamin A deficiency)

•Pasted vent (diarrhea caused by, stress, parasites, infection, liver or pancreas dysfunction, or antibiotics)

•Vomiting, diarrhea (GIT disorder, infection, spoiled food), unusual color and texture of droppings (foods eaten, indigestion, infection, stress), constipation (improper diet, dehydration)

•Ruffled feathers (respiratory infection, hypothermia, injury, egg binding, hypothyroidism, or other disease).

These are the common, but inconclusive external signs which require verification of the possible pathogens or trauma which may be present. Symptoms, such as weakness/depression, regurgitation, diarrhea or bloody droppings, loss of balance, convulsions, or shock could indicate poisoning. Your avian vet can examine your bird and carry out the medical procedures if needed, and the blood and culture testing necessary for complete diagnosis and plan of action.

## EPILOGUE

Providing our birds with natural foods and medicine, without the use of synthetics whenever possible, will undoubtedly give our birds a longer, disease-free life. We can also expect to enjoy seeing their animated zest, and their activity and productivity continue for many years. Optimum health for our birds encompasses much more than just the absence of disease. It is the presence of a vibrant, healthy, active individual, the harmony of emotions, as well as physical and mental soundness.

Nutrition directly affects growth, development, reproduction, and the well-being of a bird's physical, emotional, and mental condition. Health depends on nutrition more than any other single factor and with it comes the prevention of illness. Therefore, it is important to bear in mind that the refinement, processing, and overcooking of foods either entirely eliminates or in part, destroys the vital elements in the original substance. While most disease and illness is caused by the lack of proper nourishing foods, we can reverse many conditions of ill health through nutritional methods.

Our birds' bodies are made up of protein, carbohydrates, fat, water, vitamins, minerals, and enzymes, so it makes sense that if something is wrong with them, we begin to look for what is missing in their biological make-up to reestablish their health. We believe natural whole foods and natural medicine (whenever possible) are the remedies of choice for our future and are the raw materials for keeping our birds, and ourselves, in optimum health.

Natural preventive medicines are used in our home and in our bird facility and are given daily as a wellness plan. Depending upon our birds' special needs, an individual or pair may be treated separately on a temporary or permanent basis. Vitamin/mineral therapy, herbs and homeopathic medicines are relied upon for illness and stress.

Knowing when your birds are at their optimum state of health allows you to notice and really compare the difference when they suddenly are not acting quite themselves. This comparison is the key. Daily observation of your birds will make it easy for you to recognize your birds' "under the weather" appearance. Being prepared in advance will offer you peace of mind; while having knowledge on natural methods, offers an effective, safe, gentle, non-invasive way (in sickness and in health) of showing your birds you love them.

For more information on treatment for parrots - THE GREY PLAY ROUNDTABLE (newsletter), Maggie Wright, FDR Station, P.O. Box 1744, NYC NY 10150, 1744 (212)-888-1784.

# CHAPTER 6. RESOURCE DIRECTORY

## *Chapter 1: GENERAL DIRECTORY (for most animals)*

### *Minerals:*

**HAIR MINERAL ANALYSIS IDENTIFIES NUTRITIONAL IMBALANCES.** Hidden dangers of a toxic environment, nutritional imbalances and your pet! Did you know that the iron/copper ratio is important for prevention of anemia? Toxic metal accumulation is of great concern in pets today. Aluminum can trend to colic, muscular weakness and impaired kidney function. **BIO-SPECTRUM ANALYSIS** testing is performed using highly sophisticated detection equipment and methods to achieve the most accurate and precise results. The company provides a graphic presentation of nutritional Bio-Chemistry, and information you need for your pet to effectively utilize nutrients in turn resulting in improved energy production and health. The program is designed to precisely meet your pet's nutritional needs. BIO-SPECTRUM ANALYSIS, P.O. Box 572911. Houston, TX 77257 (800)-847-4218

**CRYSTALLOID MINERALS (electrolytes) FOR BODY AND SKIN.** Trace minerals in crystalloid form allow for greater cellular absorption. They are the key to shiny, healthy fur, good calcium absorption and a healthy disposition. **PetLyte™** puts the life force back in food and water to fortify the body's defense against chemical additives. It is a liquid blend of trace minerals in an electrolyte base **Skin-Aide™** is the first pet skin healing and nutrient spray for relief from itchy and patchy skin, infections, fungus, and to promote thicker, shiny coats on all animals. Due to its crystalloid nature, its penetrates rapidly to the deepest skin layers with minerals and a unique blend of ionically bound herbs. NATURE'S PATH., P.O. Box 7862, North Port, FL 34287 (800)-326-5772

**HIGH QUALITY PET SUPPLEMENTS.** Pet's Friend, Inc. produces potent digestive enzymes with probiotics. **Trace AniMinerals** is the only liquid ionic trace mineral supplement for pets. Ionic minerals are rapidly absorbed. They currently produce the only glandulars for pets, e.g. **Pet G.O.** wafers are a nutritious natural treat. Pet's Friend has items for everyone. Pentex negative ion generators purify the air in house, car, wherever you go. Genuine N-Zimes are potent plant source enzymes for people. **PRF** is a vegetarian live food supplement for pets and people. It strengthens the body's energy field. Microwater units restructure ordinary water into a powerful, natural antioxidant and reduces the molecular clusters for better absorption. PET'S FRIEND, INC., 5871 N. University Dr., Ste. 720, Tamarac, FL 33321 (800)-868-1009

**SEAWEEDS AND MICRONUTRIENTS FOR ALL ANIMALS.** The **SOURCE®** products supply a broad spectrum of concentrated, all-natural micronutrients derived from nature's richest storehouse, the ocean's seaweeds. As a direct processor of seaweed meal ingredients (not just a re-labeler), SOURCE, INC., has been able to develop unique harvesting and processing techniques that maximize bioavailability and result in the most potent and effective micronutrient nutritional aids available. (*see Resource Directory for Horses, Dogs, Birds*) SOURCE, INC., 101 Fowler Rd., N. Branford, CT 06471 (800)-232-2365

*Enzymes:*

**MULTIPLE ENZYME COMBINATION.** More than fifty years of research and testing have gone into creating the **VET•ZYMES** line of enzyme formulations that meet the specific nutritional needs of your dog or cat. Five formulas are available: one especially prepared for dogs, one for cats and three for special nutritional conditions. All **VET•ZYMES** formulas contain highly active concentrated plant enzymes guaranteed to be of maximum quality and nutritional effectiveness. Also available is **EQUINE ZIME,** two formulas specifically formulated for the nutritional needs of horses. ENZYMES, INC., Doug Olson, Div. Mgr., 100 NW Business Park Lane, Riverside MO 64150 (800)-637-7893, E-mail: *VETZIMES @enzymeinc, com*

**ALL-NATURAL HIGH POTENCY DIGESTIVE ENZYMES.** **PROZYME**™ is a highly concentrated blend of the most potent *plant source enzymes* available for improving digestion. **PROZYME's** formula is unique, the enzymes are *stomach acid* *stable*, making them the most effective enzymes for maxiumum absorption of every food group. **PROZYME** is scientifically proven to increase the bio-availability and absorption of vitamins, minerals, essential fatty acids and other vital nutrients, especially Zinc, Selenium, Vitamin B6 and Linoleic The increased nutrient absorption improves any pet's health, aids wound healing and provides natural relief for allergies, skin or coat problems, digestive disorders, joint difficulties, immune disorders, excessive shedding, bloating, and coprophagia. Backed by 20 yrs. of field research, **PROZYME** is beneficial and safe for dogs, cats, birds, ferrets, rabbits, horses.and exotics. PROZYME PRODUCTS, 6600 N. Lincoln Ave., Lincolnwood, IL 60645 (800)-522-5537

## *Healing Fats:*

**OMEGA 3 WITHOUT FISH OIL.** Essential fatty acids (Omega 3 & 6) are the building blocks of cell membranes and will help balance and normalize the body. Since they are processed out of most of our foods, we must use supplements. **FORTIFIED FLAX** provides these essential fatty acids with the oil in flax seed. It is nature's richest source of Omega-3 and this ground whole flax seed also contains all essential amino acids, high fiber, complex carbohydrates, vitamins and minerals. This necessary supplement comes in meal form, and therefore is easy to sprinkle on or mix into your pet's food. OMEGA-LIFE, Inc., P.O. Box 208, Brookfield WI 53008-0208 (800)-EAT-FLAX (328-3529).

## *Water:*

**WATER FILTERS FOR YOUR PET'S HEALTH.** Clean water is essential to supporting your pet's immune system. Eliminating toxins from tap water is a must, especially if you live in areas of possible well contamination and if you are hooked up to city water systems. **Aqua Belle** supplies a full line of residential water purifiers provide protection from lead, chlorine, certain bacteria, fluoride and sediment. Their extruded 4 stage carbon filters out perform carbon block and granular activated carbon filters (GAC) and come as whole house filters, countertop or under the sink point-of-use filters. This is a practical, inexpensive way to protect your pet from ill health due to water contamination. AQUA BELLE MFG. CO., P.O.Box 496, Highland Park, IL 60035 (800)-243-2790, (847)-432-8979

*Air:*

**AIR PURIFICATION SYSTEMS.** Alpine Air purification systems provide you with the most advanced technology for treating indoor air pollution. Unlike filtration systems, which attempt to draw pollution to the device, **Alpine** purification systems attack pollution at the source. Nature's *Thunderstorm Effect* is replicated by producing naturally occurring levels of ozone and ionization. Ozone will combat bacteria, viruses, mold, mildew, smoke, odors and chemical fumes. Exclusive full-home negative and positive radio-wave ionization removes dust without causing "blackwall". **Alpine** systems are CSA certified, and are proved to be safe and effective. All systems come with a money-back guarantee, three year warranty, and are made in the USA. AIR PURIFICATION SYSTEMS, 465 Buckland Hills Dr., Ste 26232, Manchester, CT 06040 toll free - (888)-203-4014

*Light:*

**FULL SPECTRUM LIGHTING.** This type of lighting is the closest to natural sunlight. It provides pet with a natural bright light and heat source that closely mimics the spectrum of natural sunlight. The extra long life **Lumichrome** bulb emits beneficial Ultraviolet rays. This type of lighting is essential to preventing depression in kennels and homes during the winter. M. PENCAR ASSOCIATES, 137-75 Geranium Ave., Flushing, NY 11355 (800)-788-5781

*Natural Remedies- Herbs, Flower Remedies, Homeopathics:*

**ORGANIC SHAMPOO AND ITCH RELIEF. SWEET SHIRLEY V® Organic Shampoo** not only cleans and displays show animals hide and hair better, but repels flying insects that disturb animals during shows. It contains Aloe Vera, Jojoba Oil, Zinc and Oil of Lemon Grass. *(See Itch-B-Gone in Just for Horses Resource)* BETHRUM RESEARCH & DEVELOPMENT, P.O. Box 3436, Galveston, TX 77552 (800)-422-2687

**TACHYONIZED PRODUCTS.** Tachyon energy, otherwise known as life force energy, is not a specific nutrient, yet it has been proven to have an integral part in the healing realm (see Chapter 1). **TACYONIZED WATER** is simple to administer. (Applying 2-15 drops directly into pet's mouth 2-3 time/day or sprinkle it onto their moist food.) **TACYONIZED SILICA GEL** has helped pets suffering from ill health, arthritis, hip dysplasia and pain. (Dosage: 2 drops on their food a.m. and p.m.). **LIFE CAPSULE** is a pendant filled with minute Tachyonized cells which are constantly attracting the balancing life force energy into your pet. (LC-M designed for pets 20# or less; LC-L for larger animals; Pooch Pouch for horses and livestock.) ADVANCED TACHYON TECHNOLOGIES, 435 Tesconi Circle, Santa Rosa CA 95401 (800)-966-9341

**HOMEOPATHIC MEDICINES AND NUTRITIONAL SUP-PLEMENTS.** For ten years, **Dr. Goodpet** has offered dog and cat owners proven homeopathic medicines that work without side effects. They are beneficial against fleas, insect bites, scratching, stress and motion sickness, diarrhea, bad breath, ear and eye problems and now arthritis. Vitamin and mineral supplements are also available for very young animals, adults and seniors. Canine and feline digestive enzymes aid the digestive process. **Dr. Goodpet PURE** shampoo is hypoallergenic, gentle and nourishing for skin. New to the line is boric acid carpet treatment for fleas, beneficial nematodes for yard fleas, a 100% vitamin C product and **"Hot Pants"**, a stain control garment for puppy "mistakes", bladder control problems, and dogs in heat. DR. GOODPET, Inglewood, CA (800)-222-9932

**"OVER-THE-COUNTER" CHINESE HERBAL FORMULAS.** Treatments available as traditional Chinese Medicine for pets use a completely natural strategy, and are safe and effective: **PetTherapy Crystal Clear** for treatment and prevention of urinary crystals and stones; **Expel** to eliminate parasites; **Calm & Easy** to sedate and calm nervous behavior; **Trauma Caps** for prior and post surgery trauma and healing; **Pain Free** to alleviate most pain. **VetTherapy** is for professional veterinary use only and includes similar formulas. HERB-CETERA, 912 Corbin Ave., New Britain, CT 06111 (860)-826-8725, E-mail: *Laurachina@AOL*

**YEW GOOD FOR ANIMALS.** Elk, Moose and Deer have regularly browsed on the bough tips of the yew tree. Dogs have been seen eagerly chewing on stray pieces of bark that fell from delivery trucks. Instinctively, these animals know how healing the yew can be. **MONTANA YEW BOUGH TIP TEA** or **TINCTURES** made from the yew are good for respiratory problems and inflammation in the legs of horses. The Indians used yew needles mixed with butter to treat skin cancer. **MONTANA YEW BOUGH TIP SALVE**, made from yew, beeswax and olive oil, can help human and canine skin problems and heal injuries. The teas and tinctures can also be given to dogs to treat respiratory afflictions. BIGHORN BOTANICALS, No 4 Bighorn Lane, Noxon, MT 59853 (406)-847-5597

**SPIRULINA FOR PETS.** Scientists in the USA, Japan, China, Russia and other countries are studying this safe blue-green algae to unlock its full potential. Current research indicates that **Spirulina** regresses tumors, prevents cancers, treats viral diseases and regulates immune system function by strengthening the body's own DNA repair processes. Fur, hair or feathers become soft and shiny. Skin irritations clear up and the skin becomes smooth and healthy. Infections may be prevented or respond better to treatments. Anemia, poisoning and immunodeficiency can be alleviated. Excellent for birds. Daily doses: Cats: Large 1 tablet, Small + kittens, 1/4 - 1/2 tablet; Dogs: Large 2-4, Medium 1-2, Small 1/2-1 tablet. EARTHRISE ANIMAL HEALTH, P.O. Box 459, Tollhouse, CA 93667 (800)-995-0681

**HERBAL SUPPLEMENT FROM INDIA. Boswella** is an Indian herbal supplement long revered as a potent anti-inflammatory and analgesic Ayurvedic source in human medicine. It effectively shrinks inflamed tissue, the underlying cause of pain, and is useful in treating arthritic conditions. Injuries in horses that have been helped with **Boswella** include chronic soreness, arthritis, stifle problems, sore backs, bowed tendons and bone spurs. Dogs and cats suffering from arthritis have also seen marked improvement from Boswella. MEGATRITION, 13610 N. Scottsdale Rd. #10251, Scottsdale, AZ 85254-4037 (800)-209-9118

160

**CAT'S CLAW FOR HEALTH.** Native people of Peru have used this herb to help humans treat tumors, arthritis, rheumatism, respiratory infections, circulatory problems, parasites, intestinal disorders, diabetes and other problems associated with a compromised immune system. **GREEN LIFE Cat's Claw** is the only cat's claw that is enhanced with crystalloid minerals to help guarantee 100% bioavailability. Cat's Claw Tea is a very useful antioxidant and all around treatment for animals during times of illness and to boost their immune systems. It is well tolerated by cats and ferrets who often vomit other herbal products. Cat's Claw is also available in capsule form, (open and sprinkle on their food.) JUNGLE PACKAGING, 4706 SW 74 Ave., Miami, FL 33155 (800)-345-1581

**HOMEOPATHIC AND FLOWER REMEDIES.** Safe alternatives to injections and drugs have been formulated by veterinarians for cats and dogs., FDA registered, cruelty-free, 100% natural homeopathic pet treatments for anxiety, arthritis, cough, flea dermatitis, gastroenteritis, hot spot dermatitis, skin and seborrhea, trauma, urinary infections and incontinence, are available from **Homeopet**. The calming essence and non-addictive effectiveness of flower remedies is well documented. These creams and liquids relieve emotional stress and imbalances, and can act as excellent first aid products. **Calming Essence®** is a five flower combination formula used for stress situations, for cuts, bruises and abrasions, etc.,. MIGHTY OAK NATURAL PRODUCTS, 10 Bayside Ave., Port Washington, NY 11050 (516)-767-3104

**HOMEOPATHIC DIGESTIVE AIDS & DETOXIFIERS.** Healing animals is simple, safe and effective with homeopathic medicine. The **NEWTON P25 Digestive Aid** is a detoxifier formula for the liver of small animals such as cats, dogs, ferrets and birds. For horses and other large animals, use the **NEWTON P11 Detoxifier.** These formulas promote general body cleansing to speed the healing process and maintain good health and can be combined with other formulas to safely treat many common ailments that affect animals today. These may include skin problems, worms, arthritis, kidney/bladder conditions, nervousness, cough and much more! It is possible to help animals get well without the lingering side effects of synthetic chemical drugs. The Detoxifier is available for people too. NEWTON LABORATORIES, INC., 2360 Rockaway Ind. Blvd., Conyers, GA 30207 (800)-448-7256 E-mail: newtrmdy@avana.net

**HOMEOPATHIC FORMULAS FOR PETS.** Just as our bodies accumulate waste and toxins over time, so do our pets. Animals are exposed to many different chemical compounds including flea treatments, flea collars, pesticides, fertilizers, food additives, water pollution and medications. These chemicals break down the animal's immune system function and internal organs leading to disease and premature death. Homeopathic remedies such as those found in *ULTRAPETS* support the gentle detoxification process preventing the accumulation of toxins. Using the *ULTRAPETS* complete line of specially formulated medicine on a daily basis improves your animal's immune system and internal organ function. This results in a happier and healthier pet with a greater resistance to disease, improved vitality and increased longevity. To order call toll free (888)-ULTRPET (858-7738) or ask for it at your local health or pet store.

**GARLIC EXTRACT.** .More than 100 scientific studies have confirmed the safety and efficacy of the world's only truly odorless garlic. **KYOLIC® AGED GARLIC EXTRACT's.**™ unique aging process brings out safer, more valuable and effective components than those in fresh raw garlic. Only **KYOLIC®** has anti-viral properties and anti-cancer activity, is truly a cell protector and helps activate the Phase II detoxifying enzymes system. **KYO-GREEN®,** an energy booster and power drink, is a pleasant tasting alkalizing green powder beverage in a food form, that puts the immune system into "over drive." It is a blend of organically grown cereal grasses (barley & wheat), Bulgarian chlorella, kelp and brown rice, full of natural vitamins, minerals and enzymes. **KYO-DOPHILUS®** and **PROBIATA,** two potent "Probiotics" necessary for optimum colon health, never need refrigeration, are heat stable, are pre-adapted to the colon and re-establish the friendly flora damaged by antibiotics and poor diet. WAKUNAGA OF AMERICA, CO., LTD., 23501 Madero, Mission Viejo, CA 92691 (800)-825-7888

*Nutritional supplementation:*

**HERBAL NUTRITIONAL YEAST FOOD SUPPLEMENT.** Scientific investigation has discovered that yeast cells are rich in optimum combinations of many essential substances such as protein, carbohydrates, minerals, trace elements, amino-acids, vitamins and enzymes. **Anima-Strath** uses specially cultivated yeast cells opened naturally by fermentation, to unleash all the valuable nutrients. It is free from artificial additives, colorings and chemical preservatives. It is proven to help build resistance to illness, increase vitality, improve appetite, promote growth and improve coat. **Anima-Strath**, available in liquid or tablets, is the ideal food supplement for cats, dogs, ferrets and birds. BIOFORCE OF AMERICA, LTD. P.O. Box 507, Kinderhook, NY 12106, (800)-445-8802

**SUPER ANTIOXIDANTS FOR PETS.** Everyday your pet battles with highly reactive *Free Radical* oxygen molecules that continuously damage their physical health and reduce their life span. BIOVET™ has combined the world's most potent antioxidant precursors, pro-vitamins, IsoSproutPlex™, natural flavorings and an organic desiccated liver supplement in their **BIOVET ANTI-OXIDANT PET WAFER™.** Vet studies have shown that this important pet supplement can reduce inflammation caused by canine hip dysplesia and its associated canine arthritis. In addition, the key active enzyme ingredient, IsoSproutPlex™ was originally developed to combat the devastating effects of feline leukemia. BioVet Antioxidant Pet Wafer™ BIOVET INTER'L Div. of AgriGenic Food Corp., 5152 Bolsa Ave., Ste 101, Huntington Beach, CA 92649 (800)-788-1084 Fax (800)-788-1083 E-mail: *Info@Agrigenic.com* Web: *www.Agrigenic.com*

**HUMAN EDIBLE, WHOLE FOODS SUPPLEMENT.** The **Missing Link SuperSupplement** for dogs, cats and horses is made with human edible, whole foods and food concentrates by special methods that stabilize the good fats, enzymes, vitamins and friendly bacteria ingredients necessary for optimum health. Users report a wide range of positive results, including relief of excessive shedding, dry skin, hot spots, doggy odor, stinky ears, wet drippy eyes, allergies, digestive problems and joint stiffness and pain. Energy levels increase in older animals, cats stop throwing up hairballs, feline acne disappears. Horses' coats develop a "spit n' shine polish, they get less joint swelling and pain, less respiratory distress, more calm, less founder and less sand colic. Animals swell less after surgery and heal faster. DESIGNING HEALTH INC., 28310 Avenue Crocker, Unit G, Valencia CA 91355 (800)-774-7387

**CEREAL GRASS SUPPLEMENTS.** Natural, whole food supplements are necessary for proper nutritional balance. Many processed pet foods are lacking the same nutrients found in **Pines Wheat Grass,** such as anti-oxidants, chlorophyll, fiber, vitamins and minerals. **Pines Wheat Grass** nutritionally resembles a dark green leafy vegetable and helps balance the high acidity, all-protein diet of most pets. The naturally occurring nutrition in **Pines Wheat Grass** should be a   part of your pet's daily diet. PINES INTER-NATIONAL, P.O. Box 1107, Lawrence, KS 66044 (800-697-4637

**NUTRITIONAL SUPPORT FOR CONNECTIVE TISSUE.** Bovine cartilage proteins or extracts, known as Proteoglycans are more concentrated than the regular bovine cartilage for the healing properties to accelerate clinical cell growth. Useful for mending torn ligaments, muscle repair, joint deformity, degeneration and skin wounds, ARTHROFLEX™ is the only product that uses bovine cartilage produced from organically fed cattle. Another fact about ARTHROFLEX™ is the greater potency in grams of active ingredients (40 to 1 against shark cartilage supplements and regular bovine cartilage products.)   LONG LIFE CATALOG COMPANY, Call toll free  for free catalog  (888)-NATURE-1

**OXYGEN ENHANCEMENT FOR PET HEALTH.** EN GARDE Health Products is a pioneer in oxygen products, oxygen enhancement and products with sublingual application. Their human product **OXY-MOXY,** sublingual respiratory oxygen enhancer, was modified for cats **(OXY-CAT),** dogs, **(OXY-DOG).** The original **OXY-MOXY** can be used on birds, horses, & fish. **DYNAMO$_2$,** a stabilized oxygen for enhanced digestion, colon cleansing and parasite control, can be used unmodified on horses and birds, and modified for dogs, **(WOO$_2$F)** and cats **(MEO$_2$W).** The world famous colon cleanser **COLOZONE,** was modified to **COLOPET,** for colon cleansing and rejuvenation. The addition of Colloidal Gold & Silver (for arthritis), make up a nutritional kit and a wonderful gift. EN GARDE HEALTH PRODUCTS, INC., PET DIVISION, 7702-10 Balboa, Van Nuys CA 91406 (800)-955-4633, to order-(818)-901-8505 SSAE #10 for catalog.

**ELECTROLYTE, "CRACKED CELL" YEAST SUP-PLEMENT.** A unique broad scope, whole food supplement uses a European slow extraction "cracked cell" yeast-culture process grown specifically for animal consumption. **PET TOTAL-LYTE™** is exceptionally high in protein which is further enchanced by the addition of electrolytes into the yeast. Protein cannot be utilized by the body unless a minimal amount of trace minerals (electrolytes) are present. The production of enzymes cannot take place without the body's electrolytes. Combined with the liquid mineral Pet-Lyte™, this protein supplement is readily absorbed and utilized. NATURE'S PATH, P.O. Box 7862, North Port, FL 34287 (800)-326-5772

**COMPLETE LINE OF HOLISTIC PRODUCTS.** Dynamite® Specialty Products has been in the animal nutrition business under ownership of the same family since 1933, offering nutritional counseling and **holistic products**. Their complete line of holistic products enhances the health and well being of dogs, cats, horses, birds, ferrets, and all other exotic animals, humans and plants. These include chelated mineral formulas, pure Ester C®, digestive aids, detoxifiers, topicals, homeopathics, all-natural shampoo and insect repellents, premium naturally-preserved foods, colloidal fertilizers and more. Used by top kennels, stables and pet owners, this company has distributor opportunities available in addition to retail product sales. DYNAMITE® SPECIALTY PRODUCTS, 310 East Watertower Lane, Meridian, ID 83642-6283 (800)-677-0919

**SPIRULINA SUPERFOOD.** Spirulina is a microalgae superfood, extremely rich in protein, mixed carotenoids, GLA, (gamma linolenic acid), and calcium-spirulan. **Spirulina Pacifica™** (grown and manufactured exclusively by Nutrex, Inc.) is the world's only certified-organic spirulina. This unique strain of spirulina platensis is grown in Hawaii, and contains up to 150% more mixed carotenoids (free-radical fighters) than any other spirulina. **Spirulina Pacifica™**

can be be fed to your pet in powder form, mixing into their food, 1 gram per day for each 10 lbs. body weight .Ths will help promote higher energy levels, silky skin and coat, and improve their immune system. Avialable in health food stores. NUTREX, INC., 73-4460 Queen Kaahumanu Hwy. Suite #102, Kailua-Kona, HI 96740 (800)-453-1187 for samples & information

**NATURE'S BEST BOTANICAL BLENDS.** Equilite Inc. and J.B.R. Body Blends are "All-Natural" unique combinations of herbs, vitamins and minerals. They are made of the highest quality ingredients without the use of chemicals or "fillers." **GarliC** contains Garlic and Vitamin C with two other chinese herbs. According to documentation, Garlic is one of the few herbs that is antibacterial, antiviral, and antifungel. **Relax-Blend** contains Valerian, Hops and Passion Flower, which when combined may be helpful to reduce nervousness, tension and anxiety in your horse. **Canine Balance** contains Garlic, Flax Seed and other Probiotic ingredients known to restore and maintain your pet's health. **Canine Flex** is a complimentary blend of ingredients known to address mobility issues. Call for free catalog and a sample issue of **The Holistic Horse.** EQUILITE AND JBR EQUINE PRODUCTS (800)-942-LITE, (800)-269-0478, (914)-693-2553

**NUTRITIONAL SUPPLEMENTS AND NEUTRACEUTICAL FORMULAS.** PET POWER, INC. specializes in natural food products based on raw, unprocessed products from the beehive. They are designed for dogs, cats, birds, ferrets, reptiles and fish. Nutritional supplements include **PET POWER Bee Pollen** and **PET POWER Trinity,** containing natural bioactive products from the beehive. Rich in enzymes, vitamins and bioflavonoids. Neutraceutical formulas include **PET POWER Cartilage Formula,** a Bee Pollen based product containing Glucosamine, Bromelain, and Superoxide Dismutase; and **PET POWER Tranquility** containing L-Tryptophan and other stress reducing nutrients. **PET POWER Propolis/Herbal Healing Salve** also available. PET POWER Inc., 3627 E. Indian School Rd., Ste. 209, Phoenix AZ 85018-5126 (800)-875-0096

**SUPER BLUE GREEN™ ALGAE.** This super food supplies nearly all the essential raw dietary nutrients that are lost in the growing and processing of most animal foods. Wild grown, raw, organic whole food. Contains virtually all the essential amino acids, vitamins, enzymes and minerals in naturally chelated form. Commonly reported benefits: increased energy, immune strengthener, resistance to infection, improvement of physical conditions, reduction of skin and food allergies, better digestion, improvement in coat, healthier hooves, better disposition. Most pets do well with just algae, but for additional support: acidophilus, bifidus, Spectrabiotic™ (a wider range of friendly bacteria), plant based enzymes, enzyme CO-Q-10, Super Sprouts and Algae (a whole food antioxidant) all containing the algae for a synergistic effect.. Independent Distributors: SHARON TRUMP & BARBARA HODGKISON, 4106 N. Scenic Hwy., Lake Wales, FL 33853 (800)-434-0889 117366

**SPECIALTY FORMULATIONS FOR DOGS, CATS, BIRDS.** Vetri-Science offers specialty nutritional formulations: for immune problems resulting in skin problems (Vetri-Liquid DMG, Vetri-DMG Tablets, Vetri-Cine); allergies (Antiox); anti-stress nutrients (Vetri-Liquid-DMG, Vetri-DMG Tablets); connective tissue support (Glyco-Flex, Nu-Cat, Cell-Advance, Multi-Source Glucosamine, Single- Source Glucosamine, Vetri-Disc, Syno-Flex); antioxidants (Cell-Advance, Antiox); vomiting and diarrhea support (Acetylator); hoof formulation (Foundation); periodontal and cardiovascular support (Co-Q10); shark cartilage (Vetri-Shark) and multiple vitamin and mineral formulations (Vetri-Plus, Nu-Cat, Canine Plus). Ask your vet for these products. VETRI-SCIENCE LABORATORIES, 20 New England Dr., Essex Junction, VT 05453 FAX (802)-878-0549

**NATURAL PET RELAXANT. Vita•Treat Pet Calm** is a natural relaxant for dogs and cats. Veterinarians recommend **Pet Calm** to relax and calm pets during stressful times such as grooming, boarding, traveling, storms and fireworks. Valerian is the main ingredient in **Pet Calm.** It has been used as a natural remedy for nervousness since ancient Greece. **Vita•Treat Acidophilus for Digestion** may help pets with gas, bad breath, indigestion, hot spots, dull coat and irritated skin. Acidophilus for Digestion comes in powder formulas for dogs and cats. Simply sprinkle it on their food everyday, to maintain good bacteria within the intestinal tract promoting good digestion and overall health. **Vita•Treat** pet care professionals produce 100% natural products for dogs, cats, birds and reptiles. VITA•TREAT, (800)-929-0418 (WA.)

**A LITTLE BIT OF EVERYTHING.** Chemical free living is what every pet hopes their owner will give them. The **Whiskers mail order catalog** and store offers a multitude of natural and holistic products from food to frisbees, halters to homeopathy and everything in between. They are dedicated to providing you with safe, non-toxic alternatives to the products you may currently be using. For a free catalog call WHISKERS, 235 E 9th St., New York, NY 10003 (800)-944-7537 or (212)-979-2532 Web: *http://choicemall.com/ whiskers*

**A COMPANY WITH COMPASSION. Wow-Bow Distributors** has the largest selection of true health biscuits for animals with special offerings for all occasions. With a world-wide reputation for providing only the very highest quality products, they promise "no additives, no compromises". **Wow-Bow Distributors** offer the finest vegetarian diets for pets available along with the purest, most humane meat-based foods. They also stock a wide variety of chemical-free items, essences of aromatherapy and homeopathic remedies for you and your pets. They believe that all animals with whom we share the earth have the right to humane treatment, to freedom from cruelty and to the health benefits that come from the kind of diet we might choose ourselves. Call for free catalog. WOW-BOW DISTRIBUTORS, 13B Lucon Dr., Deer Park, NY 11729 (800)-326-0230

**HIP AND JOINT SUPPORT. Winston's Joint Formula** was developed after extensive research and consultations with professional and holistic practitioners. It proved to be so effective at relieving symptoms of degenerative joint disorders that the Pet Project was formed to offer it to other pet owners. **Winston's Joint Formula** contains only pure and potent natural food supplements from very reputable processors. We have seen dramatic improvements in mobility with noticeable relief from pain.

Testimonials and more information is available through us directly and on the Internet. THE PET PROJECT, 505 S. Beverly Drive #428, Beverly Hills, CA 90212 (310)-277-6120 E-mail: *samf@starone.com* Internet: *http://www.thepetchannel.com*

**SPROUTS FOR YOUR PET.** Nutritional home grown sprouts are the best way to get beneficial vitamins, chlorophyll and enzymes into your animal. Easy to grow in bags or baskets, roots stay fresh and edible. From seed to salad in one week or less. **THE SPROUT HOUSE** has your answer to home sprouting. Seeds, and books on sprouting are also available. THE SPROUT HOUSE, P.O. Box 1100, Great Barrington, MA 01230 (800)-SPROUTS

## *Chapter 2 & 3:*
## *JUST FOR DOGS AND CATS AND FERRETS.*

**ORGANIC DOGGIE SNACKS. Doggie Divines** are droolicious organic doggie snacks and canine "condiments." Biscuit flavors include peanut butter and carob, apple-apricot and carrot-cinnamon. All flavors have received "four paws up" from canine taste-testers across the country. These products are made with certified organic ingredients, produced without systemic pesticides, herbicides, fungicides or petrochemical fertilizers. They are free of artificial flavors, colors, additives, preservatives, soy and animal products. There are no hidden ingredients such as sugar, partially hydrogenated oils, etc. normally found in "all-natural" dog biscuits. Available in custom-made bone shaped baskets, gift boxes, "Happy Barkday" packages and bulk boxes. BRUNZI'S BEST, INC., RR1 Box 63, Garrison, New York 10524 (914)-734-4490 E-mail:*Brunzi @highlands.com*

**RECYCLED NEWSPAPER LITTER.** Canbrands International Ltd., has been manufacturing **Yesterday's News® Cat Litter and Small Animal & Bird Bedding** from recycled newspaper since 1987. All our products are non-toxic and contain an all natural odor controlling ingredient that neutralizes ammonia on contact. **Yesterday's News®** is dust free, will not track around the house or stick to the tray and will not stain. It is extensively used in veterinary clinics and is highly recommended for the post surgical care of cats.

Besides being an excellent cat litter, it is also ideal for all types and species of small animals - rabbits, ferrets, mice, guinea pigs, gerbils, hedgehogs, reptiles and as a liner for bird cages. CANBRANDS INTERNATIONAL LTD. Sales & Marketing (800)-267-5287 E-mail: canbrand@nbnet.nb.

**PET SUPPLEMENT FOR SKIN AND COAT.** **BIO-COAT** is a concentrated biotin supplement for dogs and cats who suffer from dry skin, constant scratching, dull, thin coats and other problems often related to allergies, flea bites, old age. **BIO-COAT** is formulated in a tasty yeast-based powder rich in vitamins and minerals that is easy to feed and pets love the taste! Contains no animal by-products, artificial flavors, colors, or preservatives. NICKERS INTERNATIONAL, LTD., P.O. Box 50066, Dept. B, Staten Island, New York 10305 (800)-NICKERS (642-5377) Web. http://www.nickint.com

**VETERINARIAN DEVELOPED SUPPLEMENT.** Fit'N Frisky provides a new generation of natural nutritional supplements. Developed by veterinarians, each product contains herbal extracts and high-potency nutritional factors that work synergistically with pet foods to address specific nutrient needs of dogs and cats. **Fit'N Frisky Weight Management Program and Nutritional Supplements** combine a clinically proven herbal formula and weight loss program that results in reduced body fat without loss of muscle tissue or central nervous stimulation. **Fit'N Frisky Spice of Life** nutrient supplement contains probiotics, natural herbs and enteric-release garlic for maximum bioavailability. **Fit'N Frisky Prime of Life** antioxidants help counter detrimental effects of chemicals, environmental pollutants stress, age. FIT N' FRISKY PRODUCTS, 3011 Shannon St., Santa Ana, CA 92704 toll free (888)-348-3647 (FAX 714-444-0433)

**ALL-NATURAL BARLEY GRASS SUPPLEMENTS.** Ever wonder why dogs and cats eat grass? **Barley Dog®** and **Barley Cat™** are the "original" all-natural powdered supplements made with barley grass (grown without pesticides or chemical fertilizers), garlic, brown rice and a vegetarian-source nutritional yeast with a bacon-like flavor. Barley Cat also includes taurine and chicken liver.

Provides live enzymes, vitamins C, & E, beta-carotene, amino acids, chlorophyll, proteins, essential trace minerals and B vitamins to promote healthy skin and coat, reduce bad breath, improve digestion and restore energy levels - especially among senior animals. Sold in health food and pet stores or by calling direct. GREEN FOODS CORPORATION, Orders (800)-222-3374 (ext 434); Questions (800)-777-4430.

**RAW ENZYMES/VITAMINS IN A GRAVY MIX. NUPRO** users have had wonderful results with pets who have allergies, hot spots, arthritis, poor appetite, anemia, scratching and itching. This gravy forming mix (liver base) includes bee pollen, flaxseed, borage seed, lecithin, garlic, acidophilus, Norwegian kelp, nutritional yeast, garlic. It has no ash, sugar, fillers, preservatives or by-products and is highly recommended by many healthy pets. Their **Custom Electrolyte Formula** with balanced ratios of all minerals essential for optimum health, helps to prevent dehydration and muscle tie-ups, maintains proper fluid balance in the blood and tissues, stabilizes energy levels, combats fatigue, nausea, diarrhea and upset stomach and is good for nervous puppies. NUTRI-PET RESEARCH, INC. 8 W. Main St., Farmingdale, NJ 07727 (800)-360-3300, (908)-938-2233.

**FOODS FOR FERRETS...ONLY!** *Totally Ferret®* provides balanced and complete nutrition for all stages of a ferret's life, as determined in actual animal feeding tests. It is formulated and developed specifically for the uncommon needs of ferrets, not cats, mink or any other animal. By using chicken based protein as its primary protein source, four different fats for energy, plus the exact vitamins and minerals essential to the health and well-being of ferrets, this is the only food your ferret will ever need. *Totally Ferret®* maintains body weight, firms muscle tone, improves coat, helps achieve a higher birth rate and rears more vigorous kits. PERFORMANCE FOODS, INC. 510 Green Manor Ct., Dayton, OH 45415 (937)-890-7784

**SEAWEEDS & MICRONUTRIENTS FOR DOGS. SOURCE®** the original maintenance formula is beneficial for all breeds and ages. **SOURCE PLUS!** contains added natural ingredients of particular help for dogs suffering from coat, skin, allergy, breeding and growth problems. (*see General Resource Listing for more information*) SOURCE, INC., 101 Fowler Rd., N. Branford, CT 06471 (800)-232-2365

**WHOLESOME FOOD FOR DOGS AND CATS.** Dogs, cats and ferrets too, are *carnivores.*, A healthy diet must be based *primarily on meat.* When you can't "cook" for your animals, feed them a natural alternative. **PHD**, perfect health diet, a complete, balanced full-feed, is a wholesome, meat based diet, and a perfect supplement to the raw/natural diet advocated by many holistic vets and breeders. **PHD** has no artificial colorings, flavorings, or preservatives. **PHD** does not contain common allergens such as wheat, fish, soy, dairy, animal by-products. **PHD** has been formulated and endorsed by animal nutritionists, vets, trainers and alternative practitioners. Ingredients include chelated minerals, kelp, garlic, yeast, barley, oats, lactobacillus, acidophilus, special digestive aids and antioxidants, etc. to provide greater digestibility, less consumption, and greater well being. It is a true meat and mineral rich diet. PHD PRODUCTS INC., P.O. Box 8313, White Plains, NY 10602 (800)-PHD-1502, Fax (800)-PHD-6234

**WHOLE FOOD+ SUPPLEMENT. formulated for dogs & cats.** Like most of us, our pets eat highly processed, overcooked food. This enzyme formula provides high potency multiple enzymes to help utilize food nutrients by replacing the food enzyme activity lost in the cooking and processing of food. Each serving provides amylase, protease, lipase, cellulase and glucoamylase in a whole food base of garlic, alfalfa, barley, wheat grass, flaxseed, safflower and yeast. In addition, the beneficial micro organisms lactobacillus, acidophilus and lactobacillus planiarum are included in this product for intestinal support. Our vision is to help your dog or cat live a healthier, more energetic life through better nutrition. 2 HEARTS VISION, INC., 532 Webster St., Traverse City, MI 49686 (800)-946-6640

**NATURAL PET FOOD.** This premium pet food **Solid Gold** uses amaranth, millet and barley instead of the allergenic grains of soybeans, wheat and corn. Also Included is healthy canola and flaxseed oils in place animal and poultry fat which contributes to heart disease and cancer. Solid Gold Hund-N-Flocken dry dog food, a top seller in Germany, was introduced into the U.S. in 1974. This formula is for all **dogs**, but especially for the dog with allergies or digestive upsets. **Cat** food and **horse** products are also available. For a nearby dealer contact SOLID GOLD HEALTH PRODUCTS FOR PETS, 1483 N. Cuyamaca, El Cajon, CA 92020 (800)-DOG-HUND, E-mail: *Dane@electriciti.com*

**HERBS FOR HEALING.** Powerful results have been noted with animals, from the use of these specific herbs used to bolster the immune system and reduce toxic side effects from drugs. **Purli Natural Herbal Extracts** include Milky Oats, Skullcap, Ginkgo Biloba, Hawthorne and Lemon Balm. They also provide **OJIBWA TEA** (derived from the Essiac formula), known to be an excellent detoxifier and commonly used to support the body when under attack from critical illness such as cancer, arthritis, pancreatitis and when recovering from surgery. HERBS FOR LIFE, P.O. Box 40082, Sarasota, FL 34242 (941)-377-7400

**DR. HALLIDAY'S HIGH ENDURANCE AND HEALTH PRODUCTS.** A superb energy supplement that includes electrolyte trace minerals, silica, biotin, etc. Easy to assimilate for dogs, cats, ferrets, horses and birds. For complete product catalog: NUTRANIMAL, 7974 Parkside Ct., Jenison, MI 49428 Toll free (888)-NUTRITION (Portion of proceeds go to Save the Black Rhino Foundation)

**KEY FORMULA VITAMINS. Rx Vitamins for Pets,** formulated by Robert J. Silver, D.V.M., M.S. effectively utilize today's most advanced nutritional knowledge. Each formula provides a sophisticated combination of nutraceuticals, vitamins, minerals, herbs and amino acids and targets specific health conditions, based on scientific and clinical experience. **Healthy Pet Care** whole food concentrates, vitamins and minerals, provides nutritional support to pets of all ages and conditions. **Joint Care** features glucosamine sulfate, chondroitin sulfate, bovine tracheal cartilage and sea cucumber, nutritional support for joint cartilage. **Weight Care** with phytonutrients, minerals, lipotrophic substances & nutritional cofactors normalize metabolism and reduce weight. Rx VITAMINS INC., Attn. Craig Kisciras, 270 White Plains Rd., Eastchester, NY 10709 (800)-792-2222

Please refer to GENERAL DIRECTORY for additional information on products for DOGS & CATS from the following companies: *ALL COMPANIES LISTED*
Additional products for FERRETS
*BIOFORCE*          *NEWTON*
*NUTREX*           *PROZYME*

## *Chapter 4: JUST FOR HORSES.*

**HEALTHY HORSE NUTRITION.** The secret to good nutrition is not how many nutrients are present in a supplement, but rather how AVAILABLE they are and how efficiently they can be utilized when digested. **A.B.C.'s Plus**, pelleted feed additive is formulated to optimize the health of your horse's digestive tract. **A.B.C.'s Plus** allows for proper break down and absorption of complex nutrients with the addition of naturally occurring and beneficial microorganisms that aid in digestion and inhibit disease-causing bacteria. **A.B.C.'s Plus** also contains needed enzymes to process and deliver food properly as well as antioxidants to protect against free radical damage. Satisfied **A.B.C.'s Plus** users report reduced feed bills, better attitude, disease resistance, reduced incidences of colic and improvement in hoof development and hair coat shine ADVANCED BIOLOGICAL CONCEPTS, 301 Main St., Osco, IL 61274 (800)-373-5971

**TRACE MINERALS FOR HORSES. Pet-Lyte** (Equine Formula) is an aqueous solution of trace minerals as an aid to maintaining your horse's health. **Pet-Lyte** is a true crystalloid liquid electrolyte solution designed for total absorption to aid in body homeostasis of all animals. It is based on the human grade formula, Trace-Lyte. Also available is an all natural bug repellent for horses and dogs. **Bugs-Off** utilizes ancient naturopathic principles of herbology, combined with an electro-magnetic pH shield concept, to further enhance our pet's ability to maintain good health without employing harmful chemicals. For information and a catalog of all their products contact NATURE'S PATH., P.O. Box 7862, North Port, FL 34287 (800)-326-5772

**SEAWEEDS AND MICRONUTRIENTS FOR HORSES.** **SOURCE®** the original maintenance formula, is beneficial for all breeds and ages. The new **FOCUS™** line with added natural

174

specialty ingredients includes **FOCUS HF** (to build optimum hoof condition), **FOCUS WT** (for horses who need to gain or maintain weight under stress), and **FOCUS SR** (for the special needs of older horses). (*see General Resource Listing for more information*) SOURCE, INC., 101 Fowler Rd., N. Branford, CT 06471 (800)-232-2365

**ITCH RELIEF. ITCH-B-GONE** is effective against allergic reactions to grass, fleas, ticks and flies. It ends biting, scratching and licking, and treats associated sores and hair loss Great for dogs too. BETHRUM RESEARCH & DEVELOPMENT, P.O. Box 3436, Galveston, TX 77552 (800)-422-2687

**EQUINE SUPPLEMENT FOR HOOVES AND COAT. GEN-A-HORSE** is a concentrated biotin supplement for horses that have problem hooves, dull coats and thin manes and tails. **GEN-A-HORSE** strengthens and improves hoof growth, allowing horses to hold their shoes full term, and promotes a lustrous, healthy coat. It contains 1168 mg biotin per lb. Each serving provides the therapeutic dose of 15mg of biotin. Highly palatable. Contains no animal by-products, artificial flavors, colors or preservatives. NICKERS INTERNATIONAL, LTD., P.O. Box 50066, Dept. B., Staten Island, New York 10305 (800)-NICKERS (642-5377); Web: http://www.nickint.com.

**PRODUCTS FOR ENDURANCE HORSES.** *Performance Plus* is a special multiple blend of the most important nutrients in a balanced formula for strengthening bones, tendons and ligaments. Reduces lactic acid, improves coat condition, aids in digestion and increases energy levels in race and show horses. *Pro-Iron Plus* is a highly concentrated blood builder that increases red hemoglobin in blood to increase oxygen into the muscles preventing fatigue and soreness. *Custom Electrolyte* balanced blend of chelated minerals and amino acids is designed for quick absorption to prevent dehydration and fatigue for horses during strenuous performance. NUTRI-PET RESEARCH, INC. 8 W. Main St., Farmingdale, NJ 07727 (800)-360-3300, (908)-938-2233.

Please refer to GENERAL DIRECTORY for additional information on products for HORSES from the following companies:
*ADVANCED TACHYON          ENZYMES, INC.*

## *Chapter 5: JUST FOR BIRDS.*

**SEAWEEDS & MICRONUTRIENTS FOR BIRDS. SOURCE®** (nutritional micronutrients derived from seaweeds), has greatly benefited birds, with users reporting more intense coloration, stronger resilient feathers, improved shell strength and live hatch survival rates. (*see General Resource Listing for more information*) SOURCE, INC., 101 Fowler Rd., N. Branford, CT 06471 (800)-232-2365
**TRACE MINERALS FOR BIRDS. Pet-Lyte** is an aqueous solution of trace minerals as an aid to maintaining your bird's health. **Pet-Lyte** is a true crystalloid liquid electrolyte solution designed for total absorption to aid in body homeostasis. Add to your bird's water. NATURE'S PATH., P.O. Box 7862, North Port, FL 34287 (800)-326-5772

**ALL-NATURAL WILD BIRD FOOD.** *Wings* is the first super-premium all natural, fortified wild bird food. *Wings* was created in cooperation with (and has become the official bird food of) the National Wildlife Federation®. *Wings* is the highest quality bird food available, using only the best seeds while incorporating amino acids, antioxidants, enzymes, vitamins and minerals. *Wings* contains no artificial ingredients and no fillers like wheat, oats, rice, milo (sorghum), buckwheat, "grain products" and other undesirable fillers found in many bird food mixes. *Wings* is sold in health food stores, pet stores eco stores, select grocery stores, specialty outlets, and major drug store chains across North America. NATURAL WORLD INTERACTIONS, INC. P.O. Box 2250, Halesite, NY 11743-0687, (800)-WINGS-67, or 516-922-5987; FAX 516-922-4199

Please refer to GENERAL DIRECTORY for additional information on products for BIRDS from the following companies:
*BIOFORCE*                          *CANBRANDS*
*DESIGNING HEALTH*                  *EARTHRISE*
*NEWTON*                            *NUTREX*
*PROZYME*                           *THE SPROUT HOUSE*
Refer to the DOG & CAT DIRECTORY for *NUTRANIMAL*

# • BIBLIOGRAPHY

•*Are Your Pets Getting A Well-Balanced Meal?*, Better Nutrition, August. 1995

•Anderson, Nina & Peiper, Howard, *Are You Poisoning Your Pets?*, Safe Goods, 1995

•Balch, James M.D. Balch, Phyllis A. C.N.C. *Prescription for Nutritional Healing*, Avery Pub. Group Inc., 1990.

•Belay, A., Ota Y., Miyakawa K., Shimamatsu H., *Current knowledge on potential health benefits of Spirulina*, Journal of Applied Phycology 5:235-241, 1993

•Bell, Judith A., DVM, PHD *Ensuring proper nutrition in ferrets*, Veterinary Medicine, Dec. 1996

•Brown, L. Phillips, DVM, *Ester-C For Joint Discomfort - A Study*, Natural Pet, Nov.-Dec., 1994

•Burton Goldburg Group, *Alternative Medicine* Puyallup, Washington: Future Medicine Pub.,1993

•Chalem, Jack, *Medical Journal Document Value of Bee Propolis, Honey, and Royal Jelly*, Natural Foods Merchandiser, July 1995

•Cichoke, Dr. A.J., *The Best in Natural Pet Care*, Health Food Business, July 1995

•Coyle, Patrick G. Jr.,. *Understanding the Life of Birds*, Summitt Pub., 1987.

•Dorosz, Edmund, DVM, *Specialty Diets*, Natural Pet, Nov.-Dec. 1995

•Dunn, T.J., Jr., D.V.M., *Food For Thought*, DOGworld, April, 1995

•Dworkin, Norine, *Good Eats*, Natural Pet, Dec. 1996

•Erasmus, Udo, *Healing Fats for Animals (and us)*, Natural Pet p.36, Sep/Oct 1995

•Finn, Kathleen *Just Rinse Those Troubles Away*. Delicious Magazine, Mar. 1995, p.15.

•Fox, Susan, *Nutritional Needs of Unusual Small Animals*, Pet Business, Feb., 1995

•Garland, Anne Witte with Mothers and Others, *The Way We Grow*, Berkley Books, 1993.

•Hanger, Sylla Sheppard, *Vegetal Oils and Additives*, The Aromatherapy Practioner Reference Manual, reprinted Natural Pet, Jan/Feb 1996

•*Healthy Nutrition*, DENES Natural Pet Care Limited Advisory Svc., E Sussex, U.K.

•Holt, James S., *The Organic Foods Production Act* Organic Foods Production Association of North America, The Organic Food Alliance, 1990.

•Householder, Doug Dr., *Performance Horses need protein, but not too much.*, Journal of Equine Veterinary Science

•Jennings, J.B., *Feeding, Digestion and Assimilation in Animals*, MacMillian Press, Ltd., 1972

•Jones, Cris, *Feeding Senior Dogs*, Natural Pet, p. 57, Jan/Feb 1996

•Kirschmann, Gayla J. and Kirschmann, John D., *Nutrition Almanac*, McGraw Hill, 1996.

•Kohnke, John, B.V.Sc., R.D.A., *Feeding And Nutrition, The Making of A Champion*, Birubi Pacific, 1992

•Kostecki, Henry, D.V.M., *The Holistic Veterinary Approach to Healthy Pets*, Total Health, June 1996

•Kozlenko, Richard, DPM, Ph.D. MPH, Henson, Ronald H., *Latest Scientific Research on Spirulina: Effects on the AIDS Virus, Cancer and the Immune System*, 1996

•Leviton, Richard, *A Shot In The Dark*, Yoga Journal, May/June 1992

•Long, Cheryl Fritz, *Household Hazards, Protecting your pets from poisons*, Better Homes and Gardens, August 1992

•McCrea, Bruce, *Boswella*, Natural Pet, March/April, 1996

•McGinnis, T., *The Well Cat Book. The Classic Comprehensive Handbook of Cat Care.*, Random House, 1993

•McHattie, Grace, Your Cat Naturally, Carroll & Graf Pub., 1992

•McKay, Pat, *Reigning Cats & Dogs*, Oscar Pub., 1992

•McKay, Pat, *Have You and Your Animals Had Your Oxygen Today?*, Natural Pet, Jan/Feb., 1996

•Mendola, Kathleen Finn, *The Nutritional Value of Green Foods*, NFM's Nutrition Science News, Dec. 1996

•Moskowitz, M.D., *The Case Against Immunizations*, Journal of the American Institute of Homeopathy, National. Center for Homeopathy

•Murray, Michael T. N.D., *The Healing Power of Foods*, Prima Pub. 1993.

•*Nutrition*, Dog World, p. 25, Aug. 1994

•Olarsch, I. Gerald, N.D., *Why Minerals are so vital to Pet Health*, Natural Pet p.22. Jan/Feb 1996

•Pavia, Audry, *The Right Combinations*, Natural Pet Jul/Aug 1996

•Pitcairn, R.H., Pitcairn, S.H., *Natural Health for Dogs and Cats*, Rodale Press, 1982

•Quershi, M.A., Ali, R.A., *Spirulina platensis Exposure Enhances Macrophage Phagocytic Function In Cats*, Immunopharmacology and Immunotoxicology, 1996

• Rhodes, John, *Light, Radiation and Pet Health*, Natural Pet, May-June, 1995

• Sadler, Wm., Ph.D., *Ferret Food For Thought*, Ferrets USA, 1997

• Santillo, Humbart MH, N.D., *Food Enzymes*, Holm Press, 1993.

• Scanlan, Nancy, DVM, *The Holistic Ferret*, Natural Pet, Dec., 1996

• Seibold, R., *Cereal Grass: What's in it for You!*, Lawrence, KS: Wilderness Community Education Foundation, 1990

• *Shedding Light on "Lite" Food*, Tufts University School of Veterinary Medicine Catnip Newsletter, Vol 4, No. 8, Nov. 1996

• Silver, Robert J., DVM,MS, *Protecting Your Animal Friend From the Toxic Environment*, Natural Pet, Nov.-Dec. 1995

• Silver, Robert, J. DVM, MS, *Natural Approaches to Pet Health*, Lecture, Natural Products Expo, Sept., 1995

• Smith, Bob L.,*Organic Foods vs Supermarket Foods: Element Levels* Journal of Applied Nutrition, Vol 45, No 1,1993, pp. 35-39.

• Smith, Charlene, *Green Foods*, Natural Pet, May/June 1994

• Somer, Elizabeth M.A., R.D. *The Essential Guide to Vitamins and Minerals*, HarperCollins Pub., 1992.

• *"Source" is Best for Seaweed*, Michael Plumb's Horse Journal, Vol 3, Number 4

• Stein, Diane, *The Natural Remedy Book for Dogs & Cats*, The Crossing Press, 1994

• Steinberg, Phillip N., C.N.C., *Cat's Claw, Amazine Herbal Medicine from the Amazon*, Natural Pet, p. 34, Jan/Feb 1996

• Stockton, Susan, M.A., CRC, *Aluminum Toxicity in Animals*, Pet Trader, August 1995

• Vandergrift, Bill, Ph.D., *Nutritional Assistance For Transporting Horses*, The Holistic Horse, Issue 1, Volume 2

• Willard, Thomas R., Ph.D., *Ferret Nutrition. Selecting the Proper Food*, 1996

# OTHER BOOKS AVAILABLE FROM SAFE GOODS

*PO BOX 36, E. CANAAN CT. 06024 (860)-824-5301*

**ARE YOU POISONING YOUR PETS?**       $ 9.95
Guidebook on how your lifestyle affects the health of your pet.

**A GUIDE TO A NATURALLY HEALTH BIRD**       $ 8.95
Nutritional information for parrots and other caged birds.

**OVER 50 LOOKING 30! THE SECRETS OF STAYING YOUNG**       $ 9.95
The latest information on how to become wrinkle resistant
and fight the signs of aging.

**ALL NATURAL ANTI-AGING SKIN CARE**       $ 4.95
The newest information on keeping your skin young.

**THE ALL NATURAL ANTI-AGING DIET**       $ 4.95
Eat lots, Stay slim and avoid old age diseases

**NATURAL ALTERNATIVES FOR STRESS RELIEF**       $ 7.95
De-mystifies alternative health techniques regarding stress,
illness, focusing on flower remedies.

**A.D.D. THE NATURAL APPROACH**       $ 4.95
Alternatives to drug therapy for children and adults
with attention deficit disorder.

**PUT HEMORRHOIDS AND CONSTIPATION BEHIND YOU**       $12.95
A natural healing guide for easy, quick and lasting relief.

**THE HUMOROUS HERBALIST**       $14.95
Practical guide to leaves, flowers, roots, bark and other neat stuff

ORDER LINE (800)-903-3837
M/C VISA AMEX   Add $2.00 each book for shipping